Growing Marriage

RENÉE ELLISON

Published by Cross-Over, DBA Homeschool How-To's
Website: http://www.homeschoolhowtos.com
Email: crossover@ellison.net
Printed in the United States of America

Cover design by Erin Jones.

Library of Congress Cataloging-in-Publication Data

Ellison, Renée, 1951-
Growing marriage/ Renée Ellison.
Durango, Colo.: Homeschool How-To's, c2012.
150 p.; 22 cm.
Marriage.
Man-woman relationships.
Communication in marriage.
Husband and wife—Biblical teaching.
Wives—Religious aspects—Christianity.
Love—Religious aspects—Christianity.
Family—Biblical teaching.
Domestic relations—Biblical teaching.
HQ734 E55 2012
248.844 ELL

ISBN-10: 0974945595
ISBN-13: 978-0-9749455-9-0

DEDICATED TO...

Todd, my hubby, who taught me what "otherness" is all about. While I philosophized up in the air, he built us a secure and stable reality upon the ground. He is an icon of "tending to responsibility." And he is a master at making splendor out of the ordinary. I found him on the other end of life, too, when we encountered troubles, softly singing a hymn, steady in the faith.

And to my mother who taught me from childhood onwards to think *bigger*. At nearly 90, her life is a triumph of deeper thinking about everything from a trip to the country ("Stick at the hunt 'til you actually *find* the address or you lose all of your beginning energy"), or how to prepare for that final move into eternity ("As a believer, God is big enough to cover all of your misgivings!").

And to my father who was known by all as a man with a constant gentlemanly tender regard. He was a veritable storehouse of memorized verses and aphorisms. On my wedding day, he told me, with a twinkle in his eye, "Marriage is an adventure in adjustment!"

CONTENTS

PREFACE

Want a way to improve your marriage, without changing your circumstances one iota? Then this book is for you. Just by changing your mental fertilizer, your marriage can become something far more exciting than what you now experience. Dig your roots down deep into some different thinking and you can be flowering in new directions in no time.

Marriage is a constant process of growing and becoming something together, something that you would never become alone. Buried like two dormant bulbs in the mystery of marriage, you eventually split a crust of earth and change landscapes together. Contrary to what our culture tells us, in this book you will see that marriage is the triumph of the right kind of thinking, not of having a perfect spouse.

This book is an infusion of uplifting, sometimes mind-boggling thoughts to help you, as a wife, improve your marriage through your efforts alone. It is written by an older woman in her 60's to younger women, based on the timeless marriage principles found in Titus 2.

What would be the best book on marriage for men? We suggest *The Garden of Peace* by a Jewish Rabbi named Shalom Arush. It is by far the best men's marriage book we have ever found—and we've read many. If you give your husband a copy of that book you won't have to say much more to lay a good foundation for your marriage—it is *that* good. Some divorce court judges in Israel make it required reading before they will hear a case. Many who read it never return to finalize their divorce. This book has consistently been at the top of Israel's bestseller lists, and is now sold by many pastors in America. It is not a book for you as a wife. It was designed to be privately read by the husband.

But back to this book, the book for *you*, as a wife. Every book originates from a worldview, whether stated up front or not. This one is written from the Judeo-Christian point of view. Of all of the world views, the Bible got the human condition right. Its explanation of the world best matches what we actually see of the human condition in reality. So this book is written in light of the fact that at the beginning of creation mankind suffered a moral fall (see Genesis 2). This means we begin with the reality that mankind is not good at its source; we need a Redeemer and we need redeeming *thoughts* to guide us into a meaningful marriage and a good life. There will be effort involved in overcoming our fallen state.

In addition to bringing Biblical perspectives to this discussion, we share real life practical help within these pages. This book is authored by a wife who has had the wonderful experience of growing up under a stable marriage in her own childhood home, as did her husband. My husband's folks have now been married for over 65 years, and mine were married for over 55 years when my father passed away.

This means we saw good marriages modeled for us through thick and thin. We scooped up the "crumbs" of both sets of our parents' philosophies, attitudes, and loving deeds—even when they were unaware of it. We gleaned from them as they unconsciously dropped daily gems from the kitchen table of life, as it was lived.

Since one never arrives at a finished place of understanding what marriage even is, let alone how to live in one, we kept adding to those insights. So in addition to seeing the success of our parents' marriages, we read scores of materials, interviewed many and diverse marriage experts who deal with marital conflict as a career, and got down in the trenches with not a few women in marital crisis to walk it out with them.

We have been ever-learning and will continue to learn. We have not arrived. No marriage has. Even in the most idyllic-appearing marriages there is always room to improve. We change as people and the chapters of life change as we age, all of which impacts the marriage. Yes, even the golden older years of marriage are filled with new marital dilemmas and opportunities to grow in grace.

There have been many books written on marriage over the past several decades. No particular one of them has ever been a definitive statement that encompasses all there is to say about marriage. No one book can say it all, any more than one conversation can exhaust the discussion of outer space! So we can read each marriage book as part of an ongoing roundtable discussion about a topic steeped in profundity, one that bears looking at from many angles. Authors dive into the discussion from different shores and come up with different catches.

It is my hope that the insights found in this book will offer you yet another "go of it." May reading it be filled with many joyful "aha" moments, and offer you a fresh start of making a good marriage better.

SURVEY YOUR ACREAGE

1

WHAT IS MARRIAGE?

We simply don't know. Marriage is a part of a larger drama we all fell into and woke up in. And we cannot be too sure what part we play on that cosmic stage within the marital drama. Are we the bit player? the accomplice? the protagonist? Is marriage a drama for a heavenly host to watch? or an object lesson for ourselves? Or is every marriage a lump of clay on a potter's wheel going round and round under the skillful hands of a benevolent potter?

We simply don't know what we are, in marriage, even to each other. Are we a holy irritant, primarily a challenge to our spouse's growth? A purposeful "trouble" to our mate? Or are we the tangible representation of Christ's enduring love while on earth? We may be agents of far simpler things to our mate—an encourager of some sort, a stabilizer, a reason to get up in the morning. God is not a poor investor; He often works on multiple stories at once. Are we the main story? Or is our spouse the main story? (You mean there could be times now and then when *we* are *not* the main story? How unsettling!)

Or could God be working on both of us over quite different matters at the *same* time? We may not know the half of it!

Perhaps marriage is just a sanctification factory. Redemption was a tough job for God, but in marriage we find out that God has an ongoing taxing job of purifying and glorifying us, too! Maturing and discipling two people inside marriage *does* give them the chance to grow up all over again. Is that what it is all about?

Scripture says marriage is a mystery (Ephesians 5:32). On the practical "see-able" level, we know that marriage is comprised of a man and a woman who leave father and mother and commit themselves to each other for life. Out of this commitment flows security and children. Ta-dah—all wrapped up. Or is it? We're told from Scripture that it is also in some way a lofty picture of Christ and the church. Who knows what that is all about, really—once one gets past the ceremony. Let's see: 1 + 1 = 1—huh? How?

Marriage just might be a subtle quiet reformatory. Or even, at times, a loud one! Marriage *could* be much like the following funny scenario. Imagine you, as God, in a little one-act play. You throw your two squabbling children (a picture of two spouses) into a back bedroom (the marriage commitment) and tell them they can't come out into the larger life you have planned for them, the rodeo (or eternity), until they work it out between each other. Then you (as God) lean against the door and listen! God (you) may be shoving pages of Scripture under the door for those moments when the sparring children (spouses) get tired of each other and even tired of *themselves*

2

and cast around for something *else* to do. One or both squabbling persons might find reading someone *else's* perspective on *their duel* a relief. When the squabblers do work it out, and come out "clothed and in their right minds," linked arm and arm, applause breaks out somewhere far away amidst the stars!

Much like the walls of the bedroom in the one-act play, the spiritual fence of commitment makes us stay in the bedroom long enough to figure *something* out. Not all fences are bad. Would a blind man, for example, be more free to move about on a tiny island surrounded by alligators if he had a fence around the perimeter of the island or if he didn't have a fence to keep out the alligators? Obviously, in his blindness, he'd be far more free *with* the blessed fence. Commitment is actually one of the most freeing supposed confinements in all of life.

Commitment is scary—and to be sure, marriage is a complication. But each of us wanted that complication or we wouldn't be married. There is something tantalizing about the "other-ness" of the sexes. We were built to want that other-ness—to cock our heads and say, "How in the world could there be such a creature like you? I don't understand how you tick at all, but I still *want* you!" Someone said, "God uses the lure of sex to get us into marriage, because if we knew ahead of time how hard it would be, no-one would ever say the "I do."

Regardless of what marriage *is* in the big scheme of things, we have to somehow make it work on a practical level. We soon discover that a good marriage takes a fair bit of relinquishment of self, while learning to increasingly lay hold of an indefatigable love of someone else. Regardless of our *mate's* "performance" within marriage (how well we think he is doing or not doing), marriage just may be a chance to see what *we* are made of. God loves us through Christ for the long, long haul. Perhaps marriage gives us our own chance to have a divine experience of trying to love someone via love's longevity. Christ did it, as our example, and now, through our marriage, He may deliberately be letting us have a go at it. What will our own far smaller theater of benevolence grow to look like?

Because our culture is obsessive/compulsive on "me-isms," in its romantic movies we often see only the self-indulgence of the romantic chase. Romance is most often seen in its beginning stages in these films. The movie nearly always ends *before* marriage. In many of these films, the final scene shows a couple walking off into the sunset, with no vow in sight.

What marriage really looks like 20, 30 or 40 years into the game is left for everyone to figure out behind closed doors on their own. There is nothing in life for which we are so ill prepared.

Things we CAN know about marriage

So, in light of the fact that any person who has been married for any length of time eventually comes to realize that they don't understand what marriage even *is*, or that a spouse cannot meet all of their needs, what *can* we expect of marriage? Most would agree that we can expect a measure of: 1.) settledness, 2.) security, and 3.) sobriety.

1). Marriage helps us function in life from a position of settledness. Once married, you don't have to cast around every evening to find someone different to have dinner with, take a hike with, or sleep with. Life is settled. After marriage one can say, "This is my lot in life now; I'll make the best of it within these parameters." Marriage is a deliverance from endless relational and lifestyle possibilities that can keep one's insides in knots.

2). Marriage delivers a measure of security. Research shows that marriage is an optimal arena for sound mental health and for growing a good fiscal foundation. The security of being settled focuses the energy of life into a good progressive work ethic for the family as a whole, each in their most productive roles. When married, one is not absorbed in fleeting emotional dramas that dissipate one's limited energy. This is especially so for the man. His "have to provide for my family" mandate is the making of him. The man becomes settled at his core. Finally, marriage secures the continuation of the human race through its offspring! Now that is security!

3). And in marriage we gain a certain sobriety about ourselves. By living with another person, we face ourselves more realistically. Having to run life's details through the grid of another person helps us see objectively what we really are, not what we imagine ourselves to be. This produces spiritual depth.

Those are the basic gains. But as a bonus, even at those times when we are occupied with the revelation of how selfish we are, marriage often gives us unexpected moments of fulfillment and even ecstasy. These moments are like butterflies coming to settle on our arm. They come when we aren't focused upon them—when we aren't after trapping butterflies. Putting away the butterfly nets and stopping the hunt for fulfillment in marriage actually brings fulfillment. The altered state of our heart is that fulfillment. "At His right hand are pleasures forever more" (Psalm 16:11). Finding an unselfish heart growing inside us, through marriage, produces pleasure. Marriage may have even been rigged for this very end. Through it, God insisted on making us give out for others in order to find ourselves.

As awkward as marriage is in the beginning, by the end of their lives couples often cannot imagine life without the oneness. They may feel like vacant lots without each other. They become inseparable without even knowing it. The marriage of two people is like combining blue and yellow to create green. There is no going back to our original colors. Tightly observing and being involved in the minutiae of one other person over a lifetime expands us greatly. By escorting another all the way through life, holding each other's hands even on the edge of a last breath, our understanding of our own life is stretched.

2

MARRIAGE: A LIMITED OR VAST ACREAGE?

One of the dominant prevailing thoughts in our culture is that marriage is too limiting to commit to. The popular view is that one must shack up for awhile, with successive trial runs, in case the current mate is the wrong one or becomes unacceptable on a day when we happen to have indigestion. With more and more people choosing temporary relationships, or even four or five serial "marriages," commitment has become a scary word to some.

In reality, the exact opposite is true. Entering into marriage commitment, after applying our best rational mind to making that initial decision, forms the context in which to become fuller people. "Making the right decision" is swiftly followed by "making the decision right." Life is not only about what happens to us but how we respond to what happens to us. Being given a concrete set of problems challenges us to mature. So, too, does relating intimately with one person. Not all options are open in all realms. Math must be done with numbers; it cannot be attempted with colors. There is only one way to get to the moon; 'tis a missile or nothing; nobody can roller skate there. Likewise, we find that having our most intimate relationship limited to only one individual for a lifetime shows us something about ourselves, something that constantly jumping into and out of transient relationships does not show us.

To illustrate this point, just for fun, in the following essay we will limit ourselves to using primarily "m" words. One might say that we got married to the "m" word. We could have equally written the essay using primarily "b" words or "p" words (married someone different). Being given one specific guy is like being given primarily a list of "m" words to live with. Having to use only that list is limiting, to be sure. But if we will expand our thinking a bit about that limitation, we can easily see that the limitation is the very challenge that makes something of us. Now let's see how we do…

An essay with a limitation: using primarily "m" words…

A Marital Missive
Make up, make out and make do
Move your marriage from mediocre to *Mua*!

"Make up, make out and make do" is all about re-making *you*! When you make up your mind in your marriage to manage your own "motions" (deeds) and "e-motions," your marriage can almost miraculously migrate from mediocre to magnificent within mere months.

Since the melancholy rap is that wives can seldom manage to significantly mould a mate, should that sweet monkey *need* such a magnum-opus, most matrons quit trying. But if your marriage is less than model, even if you can't modulate a mate by mapping out his every minute, you can modify the atmosphere in which you live. You can lead by example by mustering thoughtful manners (both menial micro manners and mighty macro ones) to magnify your man. He might mirror you, if you do!

Your own magnanimous love, expressed continuously, can mount up to a monumental amount of nurturing moments, which grow to feel like living life together in a Mediterranean manor. A mollifying deep influence *can* marinate a mate, over time, but it seldom does so at the end of a mangy, pointed finger. Magpie-like manipulation will only marginalize your maverick male.

Modeling love is stronger than "maestroing" it. You can manufacture love from morning 'til moonlight when you rouse yourself out of malaise. Meditate mainly upon merciful minute, even mechanical deeds to do, as well as mega-momentous deeds like making meringue pies for your man. Maul your man with a menu of such deeds and magically something like mesmerizing music will replace any mention of a former meager messy medley between the two of you.

Yes, you alone can maneuver a melting marriage into a masterpiece "meeting-of-the-minds." A marriage can mammothly "morph" right from the words of your own mouth. Sure, it would be nice to have two of you in the mix of "maturing past the maddening moment," but if you don't have a cooperative malleable mate, re-modeling your marriage can be done even single-handedly. Conversely, malleting your man to conform to your mandates can mount up to muchas frustration. No, mamasita, be his flexible marionette, instead! To cure all of his murky moods and maladies, massage his masculinity.

Manage your own moments inside marriage and your misgivings will become minimal. Mental misery is no way to maneuver though life. Making a maximum marriage takes mental muscle. We must cast away all defeating mental musings by marshalling ourselves out of any misfit meanderings into measurable momentum in positive directions.

Meaningful life doesn't just happen. We make it happen. By making the most of it, you can do your part to transform marital mush into a marvel of mutuality. Doing so is infinitely better than living a mincing monk's life in a monastery, as a single maiden!

Why make up?

Making-up takes far less time and money than a trip to martial arts school on Mondays every month. It is far easier on the mucous lining of your digestive system. And it is faster than macho-fighting, which often materializes into a marathon. You can draft a short written manuscript that promotes understanding, later, even mail it to him, but making up *now* is expedient, and much less muddy.

Why make out?

A marriage needs many little points of connection, both off and on the mattress, to keep a marriage glued together. (Mangoes, mandrakes and mandolins manifestly help, too!) No glue; no marriage. If a relationship descends into mealtime after mealtime of a mangled maze of mediation and there is never any mocha mousse, a malcontent man may cease to be hungry for you. So, see to it that you lovingly mingle and mambo as a twosome as much as possible, in every way that you can manage. Having a consistent merry spirit can mobilize your mate to you like a magnet. By it you can monopolize the majority of his marginal emotions! If you'll "pray" like a "mantis" and memorize the manual (the Bible) you'll find the mainspring of manifold love.

Why make do?

This isn't heaven, yet. Throughout history, people who made memorable contributions to mankind were not mooching morons looking for mahogany mansions or marvy motels all the time. Such people often moved in meekness, digging in mundane places to mine their diamonds. And it is no different with maintaining a model marriage. Keep mint money management *and* seek to adapt yourself around any of your male's menacing personality flaws and the morning of your marriage will surely materialize! Instead of marital mayhem, you'll mesh, merge and meld, and the memory of your example will merit a medal.

Conclusion

If it is possible to communicate something of significance with limiting letters, as in the essay above, it is possible to do the same with the person you married, no matter *who* he is, and no matter what "limitations" (opportunities in disguise) he arrived with at the doorstep of your marriage. You can work with it. No one is an impossibility and no set of circumstances is ever a dead end with God still in his heaven.

3

COMMITMENT OR CHAOS?

Sometimes divorce is necessary to avoid getting shot, or to avoid physical abuse, or to get away from the devastating scenes of alcoholism or a man trapped in pornography or serial affairs. But what is wrong in our culture is that the great majority of young people are now *beginning* their relationships with this escape hatch firmly in place in their psyches. Marriage today is more an experience of tucking a gorgeous wedding under one's belt rather than a plunge into the Amazon with a one-way ticket on a canoe. In contrast, early missionaries were at peace with the confines of commitment, as seen by their common practice of packing their belongings in their *coffins*. They were bent on staying on the foreign field, regardless of what they might find there. They believed God to be sufficient for anything that lay ahead.

The young are so out of control on this issue, that we know of one gal who got her divorce out of the way early, in her marriage, and now continues to live with her divorced spouse, paper in hand in case there is an "iffy" day ahead somewhere. She did, right away, what she imagined would be the inevitable, just to make sure it got done. In today's world all too often inconvenience, incompatibility and selfishness are the default settings for obtaining divorces. No-fault divorce was only the legal accommodation for what was already brewing in the heart of the culture.

Remarriage is another issue altogether. Believers have all manner of different perspectives on this issue. We'll leave that one with the theologians. But everyone must become their *own* theologian when they are facing their *own* lives after a divorce. It seems prudent that a long, penetrating look at *all* the scriptures from Genesis to Revelation that mention remarriage should be all stacked up and prayerfully analyzed *before* a subsequent suitor shows up.

But back to an understanding of commitment. Many books are out now exposing the divorce myth. It is becoming increasingly apparent that divorce did *not* solve all of our problems. It did not yield the settled happiness couples were hoping for. They found, instead, that it meant trading one set of problems for another and that the first spouse didn't just cease to exist, as they had hoped. The original spouses are still re-emerging in their lives at the holidays and for ongoing decisions regarding the children. Both spouses take on crushing financial loads by supporting two households now instead of one. And they often have to battle with their own ragged unresolved past that keeps surfacing in unsuspecting places of the heart. They can sometimes find themselves waking up in the middle of the night, shadowboxing guilt, low self-esteem, rejection, or failure.

Regardless of our past, or where we find ourselves now, in a warbling moral world, all of us need to come to terms with what commitment actually means. In reading some history in *Plutarch's Lives* (Plutarch is the renowned early historian who wrote biographies of great Greek and Roman heroes), we noticed a single sentence that is striking about divorce. It says that in the first 200 years of the Roman Empire there was not a single divorce. How could that be? It is clear that in the beginning, the Roman Empire was established on a foundation of self-denial and perseverance. The extensive roadwork, still standing in some of the old empire today, is testimony to it. That same empire toppled much later, caving in to the effects of rampant sin. One can see the course of Rome's fall even in the minting of their coinage. The early coins had highly developed artwork, much detail, very refined. The later coinage looked sloppy, as if it were quickly produced for function only. So, too, we see the disintegration of their marriages.

We have seen that same progression in our own American culture. America was established and founded on self-denial and perseverance but now has fallen to the level of greed and self-indulgence. Look at the current redesigned U.S. greenbacks and compare them with the pre-1998 versions. Note the staggering loss of detail. And so went our marriages.

It is interesting that there *was* divorce before the establishment of the Roman Empire. We read about it in the Scriptures. In Moses' day he allowed divorce. It says in Matthew that Moses required a certificate of divorce to be made out, but only because of the hardness of their hearts. It is clear that the sin nature had not changed from the time of Moses to the time of the Roman Empire. So what took place in Rome had to have been a feat of tremendous moral resolve.

Sadly, we have lost our moral resolve in our present culture. The value of perseverance has been replaced with the value of personal comfort.

What the modern wedding vow really says is, "I'll stay married to you as long as I'm feeling good in the relationship. If you cause me any pain, I want out." Couples still vow to remain faithful to one another "until death do us part"—but often it would seem the words are being spoken only because of a sentimental attachment to traditional verbiage. The words are still there, but often the resolve is gone.

There are two paramount reasons for staying committed in our marriages rather than opting for divorce, if at all possible. The first is that we have made a vow to God; the second is that our faithfulness shows the world what God's faithfulness is like. It is very important to Him that we do not destroy that picture. He says it twice. In Matthew 19:6: "What God has joined together let no man put asunder," and in Malachi 2:16: "I hate divorce."

Let's analyze the first reason for staying committed—that of making a vow to God. In Matthew 5:33 it says "Do not break your oaths, but keep the oaths you have made to the LORD." The reason for this is that your words are you. When you offer your words to God, you offer yourself. Your words are the highway you lay down; they are the roads upon which you travel.

That is in fact how your very salvation is accomplished. "If you believe in your heart and say with your mouth, you shall be saved" (Romans 10:10). By your words you are translated from the kingdom of darkness to the kingdom of light—because it is assumed that your words are an extension of your heart. "Out of the abundance of the heart the mouth speaketh" (Matthew 12:34 KJV).

When you break your simple word, you can begin to unravel at your core. You have to begin adding words to validate your flawed identity. "No, this time I really, really mean it." The LORD said, "Let your yes be yes and your no be no" (Matthew 5:37). The more words and qualifiers you add, the more you have begun to disintegrate. Someone said, true followers of Christ are the only people in this world who put such a high value on their word and on The Word, and rightly so, because God called His own Son the Word.

One must not then make a vow to God lightly. In fact, my husband and I have decided that we will not make a vow at all under any circumstances other than the one to God (to accept his salvation and become a Follower of Him) and to each other (to stay married). The reason is that we know our flesh. If a pastor in a church service asks the congregation to commit to spending quality time with the LORD every morning and asks them to vow it by standing up or raising your hand, the majority of the church will raise their hands or stand up. Everyone knows that 90% of the people in that room will not be able to fulfill those vows, and yet they have vowed with their hand and with their life that they will. The ensuing guilt begins to unravel a person. It would be much better to not vow but just *do* the daily devotions as frequently as possible!

Making a vow to God is a very serious matter. It should not be entered into lightly. We simply do not know what the cost of it will be to us for all eternity. Consider this in Scripture in Numbers 23:19 about God's own view of His word: "God is not a man that He should lie, nor a son of man that He should change his mind. Does He speak and then not act? Does He promise and not fulfill?"

The very idea of God promising and then not fulfilling destroys our view of God. God is His word. His word is Him. But we don't see such value placed on the words of *people* in our modern culture. Our word is spoken carelessly and our life has trouble keeping up. Our guilt gets crusted over with more guilt, as we often act contrary to what our words promise.

So when you say the vow to God and your husband, "til death do us part," saddle in for the long haul. Let not your mind waver on the point. Set it in moral concrete.

James Dobson's father took his marriage vow very seriously. At one of his seminars, Dobson spoke of his father's commitment. He read a letter written to his mother from his father, in which his dad said, "I realize that my lifetime commitment to you might involve my suffering extreme mental anguish if you were to change in many ways, but I have resolved and committed in my vow before God that I will stay with you until death do us part."

The same is true of many of our forefathers. They viewed their word as their bond. On the Declaration of Independence and the U.S. Constitution they pledged their lives, their fortunes and their sacred honor. And if you follow their lives through, you will realize that their lives matched their words. Nearly every father of our country lost his life and/or his fortune for that cause.

To help us visualize what this looks like, there are several books/DVDs of stories that show this commitment extremely well. They are worth viewing to fortify your emotional resolve behind your good mental resolves to stick with your vows. The moral worth of these old films is tremendous. As a quick aside, keep in mind that if you opt for the film instead of the book version in any of these cases, keep yourself on a short media leash to avoid seeing more "*not*-so- good" movies.

Morally virtuous films are almost never produced now and simply cannot be produced now out of our mainstream culture. The slippery morality that brainwashes and dominates those film-makers and script writers, all of whom have been raised in our current amoral educational systems, makes it almost impossible. It takes an accumulation of several generations of moral virtue to come to the depth depicted in these films. Most of the present secular film industry seems to be bankrupt in that regard. To get one salient, slightly redeeming moment you may wade through hours of moral muck. Even if the story turns out all right, the secondary messages you get along the way are the dangerous ones. You will learn how to fight with your husband. You'll see it done and, sadly, in time, you'll find yourself doing it.

It is in that context then that we offer the names of these five books/films to you. They will help restore resolve to your vows.

The first is the old classic *Jane Eyre*. It's the story of a married man who felt himself falling in love with his housekeeper. He did not consummate that second love. The housekeeper and he separated. His wife was currently living in the upstairs attic as a recluse, having gone "mad" years before. The man was committed to that wife—even in her insane state—until her death.

The second is *Random Harvest*, the story of a woman who continues to love her husband even after he has lost his memory. He forgets that she was his wife. She is a Holy Spirit figure as she patiently woos him back.

The original older version of *An Affair to Remember*. The word affair in this film is not like the affairs we hear about today. This one is a gripping portrayal of self-sacrifice in *one* love relationship.

The Robe and *Ben Hur*, two classics set in the time of Christ, show us what committed love looks like in the midst of world changing upheaval.

Now let's go to our forefathers for more examples. Two presidents in particular loved their wives resolutely for nearly half a century. World Magazine published a stunning commentary on the committed marriages of George Washington and Andrew Jackson ("Presidential Lockets," June 6, 1998).

Other famous marriages, too, are noteworthy in this regard. Abraham Lincoln's wife was reported to have gone crazy. She became disturbed some time during the Civil War stress. She would do unusual things like order twenty-one pairs of white gloves from a catalog. She would come out to the battlefield in a carriage where the war was raging and batter Lincoln with rash words. He would respond gently, saying such things as, "Come dear, you are tired" and would tenderly take her arm while walking her back to the carriage. He endured many years of trauma with her, and remained faithful to her until his death.

Here is another case of commitment. My father had a friend whose wife was mentally deranged. They had four children. She would stay in bed all day, claiming that she saw spirits creeping in under the door and floating on the floor. She would rage at him now and then, and beat upon his chest. He was a devout believer, stayed constant to her, and asked the LORD to deliver him, content not to work his own deliverance. He was much like David dealing with King Saul's madness. Saul clearly wanted to destroy David, yet when David came close enough to kill Saul he would not work his own deliverance, but instead waited for God to do it at a later date in His own way. In both of these cases the men turned away from the temptation to rid their lives of the complication. God watched this faithfulness and delivered them with His own hand.

In another true story of a committed marriage, a Christian woman was married to a famous Olympic TV announcer. This man was so self-centered, he didn't even know the name of the school his wife taught at. Over time, he had an affair with a 23-year-old. But through it his wife stayed true to her vow. She taught her children to pray for him and she witnessed to the young adulteress about the love of the Savior. She did not set her affections on any other man, but continued in deep prayer for him, even after he divorced her. She turned her energies into running a very successful and lively Christian bookstore.

Another woman who was married to a harsh drunk of a man remained faithful to him. The worse he got, the sweeter she became. In the end she had a strong ministry in many others' lives because of her victory in letting the LORD overcome and carry her in her hard situation, day by day.

So again, the first reason we must resolve in our heart not to divorce, if at all possible, is that we have made a vow to God. The exceptions are an ongoing established adultery (many marriages have recovered from single incidents of adultery) or physical danger (but even there we can separate physically but remain constant in the heart). The original design was for us to stay committed to our marriage until death (1 Corinthians 7).

The second reason is that it will glorify God. By our remaining faithful we demonstrate the faithfulness of God to a pagan world. If there are irresolvable problems in your marriage, let you, as the more mature believer, try not to *initiate* a divorce, even if you must separate for safety. If the other one chooses to leave, that is God's deliverance for you. But try not to initiate it. It is so much better if you let God sovereignly do it. I know a woman who prayed for her husband for years and then got frustrated and left him the very hour that he was becoming a Christian. Tragic.

The greatest picture of God's own faithfulness is, of course, to his own people, Israel. Probably the most graphic story/portrayal of devoted love against all odds is this one written up in the book of Hosea. It was shared as a picture of God's own love for Israel. The prophet, Hosea's, wife becomes a harlot who goes out repeatedly and commits the sin of adultery. And yet Hosea (God) woos her in the wilderness to return to him. God is undaunted by her going after other lovers. This is the supreme picture of devotion and faithfulness that God required of Himself, even in the instance of the one area where He granted us permission to divorce: that is, if there was adultery present.

When considering the Scripture "whoever marries a divorced woman commits adultery" (Matthew 5:32), the LORD may have wanted to put down the hope of remarriage because of what it would do to our resolve about our first marriages. If there were no hope of remarriage, the divorce rate would go way down. Without a doubt, the hope of remarriage sabotages God's plan for us to reconcile with the existing spouse.

Here is a case in point. Years after a divorce, a young wife began to soften and long for her ex-husband again. Sadly, he was involved with another woman at the time when that longing began to surface. So his ex-wife moved on and became involved with another man. In the meantime, her ex-husband's involvement with the other woman fizzled and he began to long for his first wife, but unfortunately she had now married another man. So there were two points there in which there was the potential for reconciliation.

If they had remained uninvolved, their original marriage could have been restored and joy could have entered again into the hearts of their children.

Another marriage was restored after 15 years and now the couple does a profound job of marital counseling. They work as a powerful team. This example flies in the face of conventional thought that everything must be patched up in the next week. Short-sighted women say, "I've given him six whole months! Surely the problem should have come around by now." This couple worked for 15 *years* on restoration.

Another true story is of a wife who discovered her husband in an adulterous relationship. After the wife confronted her husband he initially cautiously repented. Then the husband and wife sat down together and phoned the other woman to say that it was all over. After that, the husband broke down completely in front of his wife, weeping, now fully repentant, saying, "Whew, talk about deliverance!" They stayed married and continue today in love and renewed discipleship, with three emotionally intact children.

So settle now in your mind forever that there will be only one man in your life and heart. Determine now that there is no other man. If you're going to have a great love affair in life, you'll have to have it with the man you've got.

God has said in the Psalms "He gave them their heart's desire but He sent leanness to their soul" (Psalm 106:15). If you jump ship to be with another man, you may *think* you'll have your heart's desire but you may just trade problems—and may potentially find leanness in your soul. Lots of other men may look better superficially to you, but if you really understand the sin nature, you'll know that every man (and woman) has clay feet. The second spouse's sinful nature will sooner or later come out behind closed doors. It may take some time to surface, but it is there. If such a course is chosen, personal spiritual power may lessen significantly.

Often the more a spouse suffers, by staying *in* the marriage, the stronger their spiritual life becomes. They may find a large area of ministry opens up as they are used of God more and more to share spiritual insight to help others bear their problems better.

Even if a woman finds herself in a highly physically abusive situation, it may be necessary to separate for safety's sake but as we mentioned before she can still remain constant in prayer, setting herself like a flint to be the avenue of redemption for that wayward spouse. Isn't that what happened in Dostoyevsky's great old Russian classic, *Crime and Punishment*? In that epic novel we see a man who murdered and didn't confess it. Page after page shows his mind unraveling. (Dostoyevsky does it so masterfully that the reader gets depressed just reading it.) But Sonja, who loves him, makes him eventually face his sin and turn himself in to the Russian authorities.

But when he is sent to a Siberian prison camp, she goes with him to care for him, bringing him food from afar, talking with him over the fence, encouraging him with her words. This story is such a picture of Christ, who at first tells us we're awful, and then solves our problem with His own blood and companionship.

It is good to remind ourselves, too, that no matter how hard we have it, this is not the *only* life. Eternity is the *lasting* life. Being sexually involved is not a necessity for life. Think of Mother Teresa who never married. And there are many others. Consider the apostle Paul. He may have had a wife at some point, but lived the later part of his life without one.

Some theologians think that he had to have been married to be a Pharisee. It could be that after he was converted, his wife probably left him. Apparently he chose the route of not looking for another wife. He was settled on the point. Given his prayer life, we can only imagine the degree to which he prayed for his unregenerate wife. Knowing how Paul prayed for *all* men, we may even see his wife in heaven, to our great surprise!

Personal happiness via marriage is not the end-all, be-all goal of our life. The development of character is. And nothing produces it like commitment, even if that commitment involves suffering.

Divorce is prevalent in our day, and it wasn't unknown in the time of Moses, but let us not *begin* there. Legal divorces may be necessary to stop the spread of sexually transmitted disease or to halt laundering someone's righteous money on a spouse's sin traffic, but that is different from divorce of the *heart*. Instead, a loyal spouse prays for a stumbling sinner mate. Let us ask ourselves, "Have we loved unto blood? Have we loved *our* spouse like Christ loved *His*?

What would be the matter with continuing to pray for a husband in prison for a lifetime? Are we so much better? Does love have limits? George Mueller prayed for several people for decades who were converted *after* he died! Despite our pasts, let us go forward as a people who understand commitment—and who understand the exhaustless nature of real love.

4

YOUR MATE: AN ENTIRE CONTINENT

One of the big surprises about marriage is how complex it is to relate to another human being, sometimes 24/7, for years on end. Given that intensity, even if one's spouse were Romeo or Juliet, conflict of all kinds is inevitable. Romeo and Juliet only related for one week, and look at what happened to them! If they had just skipped the balcony scene, that might have saved their lives! But the object of life is not to skip the balcony scenes, or even to stay alive. It is to live life well while we live it.

There is enough emotional geography inside each and every man to render him as complex as an entire continent. To explore any person, let alone one's spouse, can take more energy than the combined efforts of De Soto, Vasco De Gama and Magellan. Exploration of land takes all one's physical energy; relational exploration takes energy of mind. The terra firma kind can be conquered and fully mapped out in six months; the relational kind, never!

Understanding that you are dealing with a continent and not a backyard garden (or a gadget you purchased) is a tremendous starting place.

Humans carry baggage of all types with them, from the womb onwards through life. They arrive with that baggage to plunk down on the front steps of marriage, before marriage even begins. Some carry fastidious baggage; some carry bags of chaos. Some arrive with social savvy, others with escapism. Some come with demanding stomachs, some with demanding psyches, some with dripping sentimentalism, some with raised eyebrows, others with checkbook phobias, mechanical manias, strong egos, hyper-talkativeness, or dysfunctional shyness. And that is just the visible part that we can see. A brain comes TO marriage with truckloads of prior programming about all of life. Personhood is certainly very established before any wedding takes place. People are generally a complex jungle, a wee bit of a mess, before they even add a second person to their lives!

Alienation

Relating well is hard work. Every married person feels it. But why does it have to be *this* hard? What happened to make it so hard? From the get-go, every person fell out of focus at the Fall (Genesis 2). Figuring out how relationships are supposed to work in marriage, given two out-of-focus people, is much like looking through an out-of-focus kaleidoscope (the kind where you turn the cone to get things *in* focus). Through *that* lens, it is apparent that people are disjointed pieces of some original beautiful pattern. People now are nothing like how they were in Paradise. Hence, we spend the rest of our lives trying to "turn" ourselves and our relationships, especially our marriages, into some semblance of what they originally were meant to be.

The alienation at the Fall was three-way. Man fell from intimacy with God, from intimacy with his spouse, and from intimacy with himself. Very soon after Creation, all relationships were "bent out of shape" and now require great effort to put them right again. Even when a person desires to pray, with *God* on the other end, a struggle exists in subduing oneself enough to attain even that communication! Each and every time serious prayer is entered into, there is a threshold to get over before intimacy with God is reconstructed. It takes some effort to launch real prayer, to get some momentum going.

Because of the Fall, people find contrariness even within themselves. There is often within us the feeling of being at cross-purposes with oneself when the immediate impulsive self struggles with the "long-term, better self." There are days when we do the exact opposite of what we set out to do, and other days when we don't understand ourselves or know our own motives at all. So, as a consequence, the alienation from one's spouse (who is undergoing the same dilemmas) can be remarkably frustrating at times.

Gender differences

On top of that core alienation which leads to an endless potential for misunderstandings, couples have a further hurdle to get through to really communicate well: the gender hurdle. Male and femaleness. One wonders on some days if one is even the same type of "being" as their spouse, feeling like a goat trying to waltz with an armadillo!

In addition to the differing sex organs, there are actual differences in the brain, and in the muscle fiber and bone matrix, for example. See Mark Gungor's YouTube video, *A Tale of Two Brains,* for a great laugh at just HOW different the genders are.

To get some idea of what the man's primary challenges are in the male/female dynamic, see Todd's letters to husbands, in the appendix. Of course, the woman's challenges will be talked about throughout the entire book. Because, after all, that IS what the book is about!

Differences in hard drives: personality wiring

And if the Genesis Fall and the male and female differences weren't enough, there is yet another alienation. People have fundamentally different wiring, which involves not only different personality types but different work styles, ways of navigating and "doing life" in general. One spouse may be primarily a right-brain thinker and the other a left-brainer, for example; or one might be a global thinker and the other a practical thinker; one an organizer, but the other a swash buckler; one loves smells, the other must have classical music; one loves people, the other ideas or projects; one is a goal-setter, the other a happy explorer/drifter type— ad infinitum.

So if you feel that communication is difficult, it *is*! You aren't just imagining the difficulty. It is really there. We begin this relationship business at a full tilt. We have to always remember to compensate for this tilt, constantly recalibrating in light of the layers of alienation we *start* with. In eternity, relating will never again be this hard. But here on earth, it is. Recognizing these hurdles exist enlarges your patience quotient. Patience and kindness are the interlocking tubes of the kaleidoscope lens that can bring your spouse into view and your marriage into harmony, time and again.

Yes, this is the *practical* long and short of *the* most successful marital key. View marriage as a lifetime exercise in growing a mature kindness through patience, and you'll be on the right road, and stay on the right road. You never can go wrong with kindness as your *only* marital formula. It'll get you through life and across the finish line. By applying it consistently, you both can even be heralded as a successful marital phenomenon!

The Rubicon of all relationships

Marriage is the Rubicon of all relationships. Every problem encountered with every human being on the planet may at one point or another surface in your own marriage, either as a passing shadow, or something that comes to roost for a while. The potential for all relational problems is present in every marriage. But in marriage there is one profound difference from all other relationships. Within marriage God gives you all the tools, dynamics, and possible healing parameters that could ever be showered upon any human trouble, not the least of which is longevity. You get a lifetime to work on any problem.

You can hug the problem away, you can dine it away, you can talk about it today and again in ten minutes and perhaps again four years from now. You can ignore it and major on other more positive things for awhile. You can jog it away. You can share books and go to seminars. You can go together to get counsel from wise people. You can pull back and watch as your temporarily-off-the-track spouse realizes the effects of his own choices in his work setting or with the children. You can talk the difficulty through together, or you can wait for the light to go on through consequences. You can endure it quietly. You can pray in more detail than you are used to asking for specific Divine guidance all along the way. Marriage is the ultimate arena for problem solving.

Given such outstanding tools, buckle down and see what *you* are made of as you work through big troubles and small. Despondency, victimization, inertia, malaise are not the stuff of *making* your life into something. Improving *you*, and taking ground in prayer, *is*. As the old hymn says, "God knows the way through the wilderness; all you have to do is follow!"

PLANT ON THE RIGHT GROUND

5

GETTING ORIENTED

When the Scriptures say that marriage is a mystery, we must believe that it *is* a mystery. While in this pilgrim state on earth we make our peace with life's imponderables!

A certain degree of orientation is helpful, however. If you think you are playing a game of volleyball, but discover that life is really a game of tennis, a change of equipment, energy, strategy, parameters, etc., is necessary. Today, a major fundamental misunderstanding is at the root of the vast majority of marital unhappiness in our culture. We are playing by rules that don't work in this game.

The media, movies, books, talk shows, and magazines in our culture have relentlessly told us that marriage is designed to satisfy our needs and rapture us into blissful emotional euphoria. We are told, via this brainwashing, to cast around and find that other piece to ourselves, our soul mate, and then ride off into the sunset to be in the arms of more of "me."

Conversely, if we were told from the "get-go" that marriage has quite a different agenda, we would assuredly have less far to crash. What if we were told that we are to cast around to find someone to love, someone to be the specific tangible object of our groping experimentations on how to love? Let us imagine that we are to pick out that person, and then go to work and see how we do. How would we feel about marriage then? What if we were told to view it as a celestial assignment? Imagine that God said: "Ready, set, go.... Return to Me in 50 years and tell Me what you discovered." Might we start off differently and go at it more resolutely? Wouldn't we have *huge* expectations for ourselves, and no expectations for the other guy?

What if this assignment also involved the possibility of frequently looking at someone who already did it, successfully? What if there were a place to go to get "clues" and cheat sheets? What if we were provided with an example of a "couple" who succeeded at this "relationship business"—not for 50 years but for eternity? What if we found somewhere in the universe a "couple" who did it harmoniously, peacefully, with humility and deference? Amazingly, we discover that this real example isn't a "couple"—it is a Trinity! Everyone knows how hard it is to get along in a threesome. Yet in the Godhead we see not one argument, but rather an endless case of honoring one another. "He who has seen Me has seen the *Father...*" (John 14:9); "Behold My beloved *Son...*" (Matthew 3:17); "I will send you the *Comforter...*" (John 16:7)—each one of the three deferring to the other one as the greatest show on earth! We find Them deflecting glory to each other, taking counsel together, doing projects together— flinging stars into place and cooking manna! What if we kept gazing in that direction for marriage inspiration, instead of burying ourselves in pity-party cultural magazines?

So let's start over. The first major shift in our thinking would be to get our needs met outside of marriage. Where? In prayer. We currently pray so little, we look like shriveled up cornflakes. We don't know the *degree* of what we've been offered. We could be soaked, bloated, and saturated with wisdom if we would but pray more! To have an on-demand possibility of unlimited conversation with God is huge. Come lay your burden *down*. Prayer is the ultimate venting station; name the frustrations, incongruities, inadequacies and dilemmas specifically and you'll find an unimagined relief. You'll find yourself, in prayer, even picking up a few unexpected tools of navigation. But even here in prayer we're not allowed a free-for-all. We are required to come with thanksgiving, and to enter His courts with praise (Psalm 100). It is as if God says, "Subdue yourself first; then I'll listen to ya." The LORD insists—both in our marriage and in prayer—that we learn to manage ourselves and to exhibit self-control at the front gate.

Aha, now we may be getting somewhere. Could it be that one of the very points of marriage is learning self-control—that the "I do" presents to us a package with built-in problems on purpose?

Lest we think self-control too difficult, let us ponder for a moment: are we ever beyond self-control? Maybe you rationalize that self-control is impossible, because "He makes me so mad." No, you allow yourself to be made mad by him. No one makes you do anything at the spirit level. We think our extremities take us beyond self-control, but do they really? Why is it then that in the middle of a tirade, we can change in an instant to answer the phone civilly! If the reward is high enough, we *can* muster it. If we were told that we would be given $10,000 for a day of never exhibiting one cross moment, or showing any hint of exasperation, we *could* throw all of our loving powers at making a success of *that* day. If we could find the power in us to be self-controlled for cash, could we not do it for crowns? There *are* rewards in eternity and they are, after all, given out over *something*!

However, given our fallen nature, it is the marathon, the fifty years, that trips us up. Enter the need for prayer. Prayer helps us get through the mystery, even when understanding how it works exceeds our grasp. Start praying. Just do it. You'll get hooked! This is the sole place of self-fulfillment. Get solid on the point. Where do I get my huge needs met? Prayer (connecting with your manufacturer) is the answer to that question. Fulfillment of our needs in prayer frees up our marriages to be all about our man instead of "me, myself and I." Prayer enables us to meet our husband's needs, free of the pressures of our own. Appealing to God in our personal needs, as they surface in marriage, grows an ability to love another human, while we ourselves are enfolded securely in the highest of loves, steeped in all the succor we shall ever need.

6

FOUR WOMANLY PREPOSITIONS

Knowing what we were created *for* has an enormous centering power over how we live. Understanding the big picture always helps us live the little picture so much better. As Believers, we know that we were created for God (see Isaiah 45), but in addition, we were created for a role in His kingdom via our gender. We are not maple trees or squash or grasshoppers—or men. We are women. And contrary to the beliefs of radical feminism, our anatomy *does* suggest what we were designed *for*. Fundamentally, we were designed to be nurturers in every setting and at every time all through our lives, from the womb to the tomb. We are the emotional recharging center for our families and all those who come in contact with us. Our sexual organs dictate that man was designed to be the initiator and woman the responder. In addition, a woman's body was designed to plant and grow and nurture other humans. Fight this design as we might, we cannot have it any other way, given the fixed anatomy God has created. Fully one half of a woman's body is filled with nurturing apparatus! So, too, her psyche.

Elisabeth Elliot did some outstanding thinking in this area. It was she who first noted the four prepositions related to how we were created, as women. As disorienting to our modern mind as these thoughts may be, our creation, as women, is all related to someone *else*. We were created *from* man, brought *to* man, named *by* man and made *for* man. We could stop right there and all go home. That is enough to meditate upon for several decades and still not "get it" all.

The orienting thought of these prepositions has helped me countless times in my own marriage in subtle ways and in big. Living for someone else has helped me cope with life in general; it has helped me linger longer with my hubby when he wants to show me something, when my impulsive self wants to run on to the next activity (*why*, by the way? just to live life *faster*?) It is this understanding that keeps the relationship in right standing, that doesn't allow for statements like "get out of *my* kitchen." Life just looks different if we consider it *his* kitchen, *his* children, *his* vision. (They are, of course, both of ours, but it helps us if we think they are his. It keeps us reverent and tender with our man.) God gave women a marvelous capacity to adapt and adjust and rebound and finesse relationships for a reason. She has social savvy for a reason. She is the vine growing around the oak, not the other way around. The oak doesn't adapt so well. Oaks have struggles that vines couldn't possibly understand. (Just finding water enough to support their super structure might be one of them!)

Cherish your man more. Frequently remind yourself of thoughts like: "I'm important to his well-being. If I do not fulfill many needs for him, his life is truncated. He simply lacks the psychological and physical support necessary to fully complete his life." Yes, determine to be whatever he needs— whether that be his cowgirl or his elegant First Lady. You were designed by God to be resilient enough to be able to become whatever your man's particular and specific "being" requires.

There are bankruptcies in a man that make him go hunting for his helpmeet in the first place. Most men know, at some deep level, that they feel incomplete without the emotional component of a wife. We are women and cannot understand this. We can live alone quite sufficiently in old age after a man dies. Not so the man. We must understand that our own female experience of life is not what the male's experience of life is. We only have a limited viewpoint. It is Scripture that opens our eyes to more points of view. God has eyes, like a bee, in every direction; we only see straight ahead. You miss a great deal if you only see straight ahead—you miss three-fourths of the world.

So what *is* the female marital challenge, in a nutshell? From a man's point of view, he desperately needs a wife who believes in him and affirms him. She accomplishes this by showing deferential respect to her husband, feeding him, and hugging him!

As anathema as this notion is to our current culture, it is *the* secret stair to enter your husband's inner man. You don't have to seek to understand complexities about him. Unlike you, he doesn't have them. He is straightforward. What he *does* care about is, is *he* noticed? Is he looked up to? His ego is fragile. He can't be a king without a kingdom. Put a kingdom *under* him by getting under him. Slow down. Seek his insight on little and big matters. Hold your own will loosely for awhile.

Eve blew it by not seeking Adam's insight; she was bent on her own immediate will. No doubt, she blew it by not being surrendered to Adam in her demeanor. It was there that she missed the boat. According to Scripture, a man *knows* what he is doing. But he is less verbally quick than a woman. Research actually shows this difference in male and female brains. It takes a man longer to frame the words, and there will be fewer of them when he does say them. So, hang back and allow him that time. Be quiet enough to really hear him. Because a woman is so verbally quick, she has a tendency to become fast-paced-intimidating in her less refined hours, becoming excessively domineering. When she shifts into this gear, a man will back out and flat withdraw. You have to *want* his input, so hog-tie, muzzle and sit on yourself long *enough* to let that happen, each and every time.

Take the matter of *hearing* your husband's insight seriously. If you don't genuinely believe that God put insight into your husband that you desperately need, you'll miss His stabilizing provision for *you*. God put something in that man that you need. No matter how articulate or wise you are, don't look down on your husband; look *up* to him as God's viceroy on the earth. Listen.

Because of his high levels of testosterone and stronger physical prowess he is not so sensitive to anxieties and stresses as you are. But he is *very* sensitive to how you treat him. It is an adulteress's adoring eyes that sweep a man into adultery. If he doesn't get such adoration from his wife, he'll be tempted to look elsewhere. So, as his wife, respect him, admire him, affirm him, refer to him, come up under him, and you'll find your husband becoming a great man. Start respecting his input in all the areas that you *can*, even if his lifestyle doesn't deserve it. Just start honoring him and watch what happens.

The reverential attitude of your heart, coupled with serving him in his physical needs, is the *sure* road to deeper oneness with your husband.

7

UNSETTLED BY HIS MASCULINITY?

Just for fun, sit back and picture your husband as he was when he was a little boy. He is now a grown-up version of that boy. He didn't morph into something else en route. As a grown-up version of the boy, he probably won't be as refined as you are. He'll be more forthright and less subtle. His irrigation boots are muddy. Athletic and work clothes are dirty. Projects mean dealing with *stuff*, and some of that stuff messes up the house. He might put his feet up on the coffee table, or take over the whole kitchen just to fry eggs, or cough too loudly or walk too loudly or talk too loudly. Or maybe he hurls the bedcovers all over the place, or leaves the bathroom in shambles. Or perhaps you deal with the opposite sort of man, the one who is such a neat freak that he comes across as rigid. You can be sure that whatever your guy does, he does it with testosterone. This is a *guy*. If you really want the *Rocky* Mountains to be the rolling plains, you're going to have some troubles adjusting to reality. You can't insist on structures or behaviors that aren't in line with the essence of the original thing. You can't have reality both ways.

So, run your fingers through his short croppy hair, especially the boy part that sticks straight up, while you sleep next to him—and enjoy it! If he wears boots to bed, love those boots, too. Love his tools and projects; love the fact that there is a man around the house.

A man is so…physical. A large part of his well-being is satisfied in the physical realm. Feed him frequent food and be available and warm to him physically and he will be quite satisfied. A simple, highly repetitive and predictable home routine and setting satisfies most men immensely. And if you add a little cheerfulness as you go about your home-making and your lovemaking he'll feel like he "died and went to heaven." You are a nurturer to your hus-band, not just to your children. Look at him with loving warm *eyes* while you work. Deliberately sof-ten those eyes. You'll be delighted with the response you'll get.

When we were first married, I was privately incredulous at my hubby's repeated need to tell me his dreams or what he ate at a meal when he was away from home. I thought to myself, quietly, "It doesn't change *real* life one whit, and what does it *matter*?" until I heard that the famous violinist Isaac Stern's wife has to listen to what he eats at his meals away from home after his worldwide concerts!!! *Oh*, I get it—it is a guy-thing. And many issues *are*! Saddle up. Smile.

Then, move past the "boy part" and respect him as a man. A man isn't just a grown-up boy, any more than you are just a grown-up girl. Something profound happens during the transition into adulthood. It is something God does *to* a man—even if the man doesn't notice it happening to himself. When a boy becomes a man, there is a mysterious something that transpires between God and the man. He is supernaturally and quietly vested with very clear moral vision and the authority to lead his family. This office given to him from heaven is real. Men have clearer moral vision than women, even when they themselves are sinning. A woman, on the other hand, may have clouded judgment from emotional factors or rationalizations. (By the way, rationalization is supplying reasons for what your spirit knows is wrong.) Eve "reasoned." Issues can get cloudy in a hurry for women who are overly governed by their emotions or by extra room in their female brains for "exciting possibilities."

"And Adam was not the one deceived; it was the woman who was deceived" (1 Timothy 2:14).

Think of it: Adam, as her head, could have been Eve's mediator instead of her accomplice. He could have even bravely killed the snake! He saw the issues, clearly. The human race did not fall just from Eve's action—the Fall took place when Adam joined her. 1 Corinthians 15:22 confirms this: "In *Adam* [*not Eve*] we all die." So, recognize that there is more going on in marriage than having a man at your side; he is a heavenly representative of divine government.

Respect the standing of your husband before God, and speak to him with a high regard. Don't talk over him or past him. Get *under* him and *beside* him.

8

THE SCARY "S" WORD: SUBMISSION

There is almost no word more explosive in our modern world than the word submission. Our flesh hates it and the world is only too ready to rush in with rationale to support our own tendencies to resist it at all costs.

Throughout history the Enemy has commandeered certain words as emotionally loaded trigger points over many issues in life. It is no different now. He uses slippery words to usher in his entire agenda for our demise. The clever words of pro-choice in the abortion debate are, in reality, pro-murder. So, too, he coined words for the radical feminists' agenda, which he birthed in order to break down the home.

Note the downward spiral of the feminists' migrating thoughts here. At first the radical feminists said, "I will not submit to a man for any reason." But, then, not so far down the road, this turned into defiance of even a good man, and eventually into despising all men. She began saying "I'm not really after equality; I wish to be *better* than a man. And come to think of it, I don't need a man at all, I will be a homosexual." If we *all* were homosexuals, the procreation of the race would cease. It is a death agenda.

And so it is with the word "submission." Both the abortion argument and the feminist agenda's argument are framed around frail threads, the rare case. Abortion is excused on the grounds of the rare case of rape, but is largely executed for issues of convenience: an unwanted gender or physical disability of the unborn child. Something that rarely happens has become the excuse for murdering normal babies—40 *million* all told (register fully that this is not a small result)—and brazen harvesting of baby cells for commercial purposes. The Enemy fed us the "rationalities" to do what our flesh *wanted*—which is to end the life of any inconvenient child.

So, too, he has a contentious/combative agenda for the husband-wife relationship, through radical feminist brainwashing, which he framed around the case of fighting for *wage* equality, when really he was fighting for *identity* equality. His true aim was to attempt to destroy sexual differences altogether. He was configuring a sexual agenda against reality, re-ordering reality in direct defiance of God's original design in the Garden. The ultimate goal? Destroy the family.

The Enemy started by attacking the issue of submission. He hurled confusion into the fray by implying that the submission scriptures of Ephesians 5:21-24 were given as a weapon to men to lord it over women. But if we examine the scripture closely we see that the injunction of submission *was never given to the man.* It was given to the woman. It is a voluntary humble posture she assumes in relation to her husband each and every time she chooses to employ it for peace in the home. The man was only told to love her. So the Enemy seeks to make us despise God's ways by fomenting an outrage over something that never was even written in Scripture.

A man is not given the authority to make a robot out of a woman. Submission is a private grace that a spiritually maturing woman learns to employ in response to *God's* will, not a husband's demand. She understands that via this grace, God miraculously makes one set of circumstances work out for *two* people, to the good of them *both*! Further, she understands that God works directly behind the husband's decisions to bring about good for the total family—good that the husband might not even fully intend, know about, or understand. So she assumes this posture quickly and readily in as many daily issues as she can. A larger impasse may require a fair bit of good discussion between her husband and herself, but the final course of action is the responsibility of the man if agreement cannot be reached. (Such an instance is a rare case in most marriages. Usually, increased discussion clarifies the wise course for both man and wife.) She volunteers this spirit first as a love gift to God, and secondly as an avenue to bring balm and blessing to her husband and the family. Submission loses all its power if it is arm-wrestled out of a person. Robotic love simply doesn't work. Robotic love is dead love.

A case of the overbearing man in sin

Submission is a helpful grace in a normal marriage, but what of the case of a man who is way out of line, deep in sin? Consider this: when the same act is committed in rape as in the marriage bed, what makes one a crime and the other a glory? Answer? The presence or absence of consent! Mutuality is missing, in the case of rape. Any time a person is doing something to another person against their will, it is way off base. If there is coercion, physical beating, verbal abuse, arm-twisting, blackmail, oppression, etc., this is an entirely different matter. Let us be very clear here. Throwing lamps, molesting children, banging someone's head against the wall, causing people fear by entering into a room—none of these are acceptable human behavior. Accountability needs to be brought to such a man. Go get help.

The great majority of submission squabbles, however, are over *preferences*. And these you may easily give in to with absolutely no fear of damage to your soul, with the sure result that you will add to the harmony of your home in a big way. A gentle and quiet spirit is of great value in God's sight. Regardless of what radical feminists think about it, it is on *God's* radar. You bring pleasure to God by being lovely in this way. He counts on you to be a soft place in His universe and to render a good picture of the tender part of His nature to those on earth. Endless arguing destroys that picture, and brings unbearable tension into the home.

Submission is not an absurd word. It is a life-giving word when entered into with grace. An orchestra simply cannot function without all of its members submitting to a director so that they can go ahead and make music together. The point of life is not about who wins an endless tussle over rule and subjection. We need to get beyond that in order to take unified, harmonious dominion over life's exciting possibilities. A couple in a parking lot could choose to endlessly fight over who will drive and never get in the car and go anywhere! So, too, terrorist Muslims who live solely to eradicate the Jews need to get beyond their obsession with murdering— for their *own* sakes. If they don't, they'll have a tough time deciding what to do *after* they've eradicated a significant chunk of the human race! What would they then be living *for*? Once we, as women, succeeded in getting free of "man," or neutering him through intimidation, what would we do as an entire world populated only by women? *Then* where are we?

It is impossible to waltz with two leaders. The beauty of dancing results from a combination of a leader and follower who even look very different— one partner in a formal suit, the other in billows of chiffon and crystal slippers. Witnessing the beauty of these differences waltzing smoothly across the floor takes one's breath. Likewise, in a marriage, one of the two has to lead. God has designed the husband to be that one. Headship is not up for grabs. It wasn't designed to erratically change hands, issue by issue. It is a well-ordered, well-crafted social arrangement.

Being aware of how decisions are *finally* made, doesn't exclude wholesome multi-sided discussions leading up to the moment of action. Submission is about *outcomes*, not about *input*. A woman can often help her man with additional enlarging insights that he may not be aware of. A wife can make appeals, too. Appeals acknowledge a husband's headship; amazingly, once that is acknowledged the man can actually *hear* her. A reverent attitude in relation to a man works wonders. If an issue is particularly complex, a couple can also wait, pray together, or go get counsel from spiritually older and seasoned believers. But in the end, *something* must get decided. The buck stops with the man.

Military advances would go all to ribbons if troops tried to respond to two conflicting captains shouting opposing orders simultaneously.

God is not into creating chaos or ugliness. He is not an ogre. The Enemy is always issuing bad press about God. But all brainwashing eventually meets its waterloo. Feminists accepted the Enemy's side of the debate several decades ago but now, not a few find themselves not so keen on those ideas anymore. They are exhausted with the double workloads they insisted upon bearing, carrying both the man's and the woman's roles.

Radical feminist roots

As feminism was emerging we all thought the struggle was for equal voting rights and equal pay. If that had been all it was, who wouldn't be for that? But the movement had insidious tentacles far deeper than this. Those who have defected from its insider high ranks have exposed its manifestos. The culture has begun to see an emerging reality that they hadn't counted on—a Pandora's Box. Women traded the supposed drudgery of the kitchen and the supposed oppression of their husbands for the deeper drudgery and additional stresses of the workplace. Many of these women found themselves working at minimum wage, now carrying an additional load from someone else's oppressive husband who was now her boss. And she found that her domestic load still existed; someone still had to do *that* work, too.

At the soul of the movement was the socialist/Marxist intent to remove the mothers from the home and have the state control the children. Gone would be the rugged individualism and entrepreneurial spirit spawned in children who had the full investment of their mother's attention during childhood. In the past, devoted on-task mothers had stabilized their children's personhood, resulting in a strong, productive, inventive nation. The increase of an honorable capitalism fueled by reward for hard labor began with the children's lemonade stands on the street corners. But now, with their mothers working, children could easily become wards of the state, and be schooled (reprogrammed) in dumbed-down educational institutions. The feminist leaders' end-run goal was to have modern children work for minimum wage without complaint, passively letting someone else (the state) do their thinking for them.

When women left home, eager to be the presidents of companies and countries, thinking they could do a better job than those "weakling men," they found that they had fallen into a pit. Complaining of the "suffering" of the home, they now entered into double suffering. When they woke up from their delusion they found that they had fallen under the curse of the ground, too, not just of childbearing (Genesis 2). Now they had entered the sweat of the brow in addition to the tribulation of the womb.

When the debate was originally framed that the woman needed to leave home, her job was envisioned and understood to be in terms of white collar jobs—CEO jobs, luxury jobs—but what *happened* was that women entered the work force in blue collar slave labor jobs at minimum wage as hotel room cleaners, bar maids, hairdressers, etc. Consequentially, several generations of those women's abandoned children suffered under day-care systems where they were trained by other blue-collar workers. Huh? And this was an improvement? Was it an improvement for their *children*? And even if a woman landed a CEO job, was that an improvement for *her*? Was the increased stress and missing whole chapters of her children's lives for preoccupation with other people's lives worth it? Will she get a second chance to raise her own young family again? What did it cost her, ultimately? Is she satisfied with the results?

Our culture, swayed by the feminists' slant against submission, traded the occasional suffering of some women under some excessive men at home, for double suffering of all women. Make no mistake, both are sufferings, but it's simply not the truth to believe that the Devil's way is glorious and the Biblical way utterly untenable. The Enemy always frames the godly part of the equation as absurd but his own deviant way as the way of true freedom. But when his ways are found to be *more bondage*, sometimes people grow wise and return to God's ways—but not always. Communism, even though it has been proven to bring in the greatest slaughter of the history of the human race and is responsible for over 200 million deaths under totalitarian regimes, *still* is embraced on college campuses as an improvement in government. The will of fallen man is vigorous; his eyes dart in every corner to escape the clear designs of Creation and its Maker.

Further, the effects of radical feminism on the men were equally devastating. The responsibility of providing for a family is the primary agency of civilizing a man—giving him something to live *for*. If he feels unneeded, watch him willingly exit as he has done in the ghettos all over America and England. While women are loudly voicing their opinions, watch the men. They grow quiet and slip out the back door. If the message is chronically "I don't need you," he'll remove himself. The football field and pornography have taken up the slack.

Practical application of submission

Many exhausted women now see through the feminists' empty promises and want to go back home. When they get under their man and support and encourage him, it makes an earlier heaven of their homes. There is no place on earth where your husband would rather be than with you and the children if you make it very clear that you respect him and appreciate him to the hilt. You have a choice here. The wise woman builds her house (Proverbs 14:1) and that starts with building her man. Most men will not take on an articulate woman who is on a rampage. Most would prefer to simply grow quiet. To hear what a man really thinks, *you* have to grow quiet. Ask men what they think of dominant-drill-sergeant-bossy women. For the past several decades men have been intimidated and threatened into saying nothing. But they still *think*.

As we've pointed out, most all of a woman's internal submission debates come to her over questions of *preferences*, not of the overbearing sin of a man. If a man is asking you to sin, don't submit; obey God rather than man. But if you'll submit to your husband over the great majority of questions regarding preference you'll find that a sweetness enters your home.

God is ingenious in His designs. As a woman learns to subdue her will, she becomes a gentle and quiet wonderful presence in the home, and it grows the man's ability to lead. If she takes over, her children and husband tire of her, plan mental escapes, and the husband grows lazy.

A key help for the woman is contained right inside the 1 Peter 3:1-6 passage about submission. Note the words: "Do not give way to fear." This fear is most often a fear of a loss of control, but it can be a fear of a husband's negativity or grumpiness. But your husband's way of relating to you could look mild compared to dealing with a male boss or a female boss withholding your paycheck over some trivia, or compared to the ruggedness of life in a concentration camp. This is a fallen world; there are no conflict-free zones either in the home or out there in an office with no windows, contrary to what we've been led to believe.

Wanting to share personal difficulties with an understanding listening ear at work has caused many women in the work force to fall into adultery with a married co-worker. This is not a rare scenario. This immediately compounds the working woman's guilt load. So in addition to double the stresses she may also bewilderingly find herself dealing with estrangement from God, through decisions she may regret. Perhaps she could have eventually reasoned with a temporarily harsh husband, but now can't reason at all with a boss who drinks, or one who insists on lunch together in order to get that pay raise.

Make no mistake, submission as a wife involves dying to self. Motherhood, too, is all about dying to self. It may go against our flesh to think about daily dying right on the ground (the home) where we are planted, instead of some imagined ritzy (more often a cold) office building. An acorn doesn't totally enjoy dying on the ground either. But consider the acorn's dying results! Are oaks so bad? The Bible is full of paradoxes that go against the natural mind.

See to it that respect is given

A man's psyche is vulnerable without the affirmation and respect of a woman. Therefore, "The wife must see to it that she respects her husband" (see Ephesians 5:33 NASB). Continuous counter-suggestions can be like little foxes spoiling the vine, nipping at his heels.

The wording, "see to it" that you respect your husband, implies that you make sure, hover over your responses, and possess your vessel in extra self-control in this regard. Respect is primarily expressed in tone of voice and body language. It is not only what you say but also how you say it. I told my husband once, "Well, I'll submit, but this is a harebrained idea!" He shot me a wry smile and replied, "Somehow, I don't think that's going to make it past the pearly gates, sweetie."

One cantankerous old woman viewed submission like this: she decided all of the domestic issues like where they should live, where they should go, how much they should spend. She let her husband decide all of the larger issues—like whether our country should go to war, whether we should continue outer space exploration, and who should run for public office!

You'll simply be amazed at the peace in your home if you train yourself and your daughters to quickly follow your husband's even small suggestions and wishes. Try it out with the choosing of restaurant seats and parking spaces or which part of the garden to plant first. It's a simple equation: the more frequent the submission, the more peace.

Just for fun, you might occasionally show your children what submission looks like, even in you, through an exposure of your own thought life. "What your dad has just asked me to do is inconvenient and my flesh doesn't want to do it right now. But I'm going to obey him anyway, just like you have to do with us. I choose to do this because I want to honor him and want the peace it will bring to our home. Now watch your mother get up and get what your father needs!" Later you can whisper in your hubby's ear, "Aren't I terrific!"

Speak well of your husband to your children. Put the best face on all that he does and is. You may have to get creative here. One of my friends was training her children to be kind, but her husband burst through the door with an extra dose of contrariness one evening. The kids identified it and one of them blurted out, "Mom, why does Dad get to act like that? She was quick-witted and retorted, "Well, if your dad had been raised like you, he'd be different. But he wasn't, so he doesn't. So that's that."

Similarly, one time my husband seemed overly gruff with our daughter. She came running to me for sympathy. But, having learned from my friend's example, I retorted, "Well, what did you expect? God made men that way so that they could go to war and protect us." Instead of dissolving in tears, she cocked her head for a moment, said, "Oh," and ran merrily off!

Your children can be a mirror for you to notice how well you're submitting. If they are contentious, chances are that they learned it from you. In the Scripture, contentiousness is most often connected with a woman. The dictionary shows that it simply means maintaining your side of the argument! Drop the argument. Simply drop it. Take it up at another time, if you have to, when the atmosphere isn't supercharged with who will win. The Bible says a righteous man turns away from an argument. Proverbs 20:3 states: "It is honorable for a man to stop striving, since any fool can start a quarrel." When you happen to hear bickering in other people's marriages, notice the triviality of the issue. Isn't it nearly always over some dumb thing: where to park, what date an event occurred, what it cost? Ask, "Will this really matter a year from now?"

Let it go. We see from the Scriptures that the woman is prone to keep it up, because often she is right. But to argue it down to the mat every time is a weakness to her. An old adage says, "Better to let error live, than to let love die."

It is a mandate

"Wives, submit to your own husbands, as to the LORD. For the husband is head of the wife, as also Christ is head of the church; and He is the Savior of the body. Therefore, just as the church is subject to Christ, so let the wives be to their own husbands in everything." (Ephesians 5:22-24 NKJV)

Surprisingly, because submission is a spiritual mandate, this sort of self-control and self-mastery for the lifting up of the man becomes a benefit for the woman, too. Through the exercise of it she becomes a refined, elegant woman. Subjugating oneself to the will of another is so difficult that as one progressively masters it, it produces beauty and irresistible selflessness. People throng to be with a truly loving, affirming and other-centered woman.

To respect your husband is the one command given by God to women in the Scriptures in relation to living *well* with their husbands. Our tendency is to *rule* our husbands. Notice that God gives the command to our weak side, to shore up our fallen propensities to the contrary. It is easier for us to love than to respect. Our husbands hold an office/position of authority, given them by God. And so it is that no mention is made to the woman to love (which she does naturally) but rather to respect (which is more difficult).

Watch over yourself carefully in this area. This is a timeless principle. It was an infraction of this very area that caused King Xerxes, so long ago, to deal so severely with Queen Vashti's irreverent conduct (Esther 1:18). He feared that because of her example "There would be no end of disrespect and discord throughout the realm"—not very unlike what we see in the culture today, or what God saw in His heaven with Lucifer.

As with all of God's puzzling mandates, sometimes we come to know only *after* we have obeyed (John 6:69). We come to see that God's design for authority is really for the *benefit* of those who submit to it. It will produce both supernatural *protection* and supernatural *guidance* for the woman who trustfully submits to her husband. This posture reduces her stress load. Over time the spiritually mature woman comes to see that there is a divine hand working even through her husband's seemingly unnecessary or bizarre requests that works a greater good for her. Picture a woman crying on the shore because her seemingly selfish husband won't let her board the ship, only to hear later that the ship went down. Or a frustrated husband asking his wife irrationally to go to the store *now*, only to find a clerk there who is on the verge of suicide…the whole request resulting in a divine appointment. If a woman can come to see God's eternal good will for her behind every scene, then submission begins to work a grace in her life.

Because He put the man in the position of authority in the home, God vindicates the man time and time again sometimes by making even his mistakes turn into good. God validates the office of his manly viceroys on earth. God is the God of order, not of chaos, and this includes order in the family. Matthew Henry, in his Bible commentary on Judges 20, wrote: "We may be sure of the righteousness, when we cannot see the reasons, of God's proceedings." How can we trust that God works good even when the man is not aware of it? Both Scripture and personal histories of believing women bear it out. Let me give you two examples of my own case.

Once, about 15 years ago, my husband and I had a festering recurring conflict about a mangy tree, which I thought was misplaced in the lineup of trees in our backyard. I wanted to cut down that ugly locust tree that had grown to be too tightly sand-wiched in a row of only evergreens. It clearly did not belong in there aesthetically, I reasoned. It had been planted there by a previous owner as a little sapling of a tree without thought of how it would look when grown. But my husband flatly, stub-bornly would not cut it down. He refused even the reason behind my wanting to eliminate it, apart from the work it would take to chop it down. I brooded for a while and then got occupied with other things and let the matter drop. Years later, a family bought the vacant lot behind us and built the front door of their new home right in the view line of that spot. I've been grateful for the privacy of that tree ever since!

Another time, I was taking my daughter to a mu-sic lesson and my husband told me to drive home using a certain specific route to get gas only at that station. When I was driving home I got to the final fork-in-the-road intersection and pulled over to the edge of the road as I sat there and reasoned, "This is *nuts* to go home in the direction my husband com-manded; it takes way more time, requires more miles, and only saves ten cents worth of gas—which will be used up in the extra miles to get there! This makes no sense!" I sat there hotly deliberating between obedience and rationality. In a rare moment I chose obedience! A divine appointment happened at *that* gas station, that wouldn't have happened otherwise.

By going his route, I *could* have missed being trapped in a severe accident up ahead. We can learn to have a high regard for what might be God's workings *behind* our husbands' seemingly irrational or stubborn decisions that we cannot see now. We simply are not God. We do not see every angle of a situation.

If submission entails some suffering, suffering under the hand of God's sovereignty is not wasted. 1 Peter 5:10 offers this encouragement: "But may the God of all grace, who called us to His eternal glory by Christ Jesus, after you have suffered a while, perfect, establish, strengthen, and settle you." To the contrary, suffering for our own willfulness, in direct defiance of God's ways, is not so blessed. We can find ourselves in conditions that are worse than submission to a husband's mere preferences in this world.

When it is an issue that really matters to you, appeal to your husband's authority in a sweet spirit of submission, acknowledging that his authority exists. This leaves your husband's esteem and position intact. His perhaps thoughtless "no" might easily be reversed in such an atmosphere. Humble deference to a husband is always in order and just may be the way of acquiring your own real beauty. It certainly was for Abigail who appealed to David's own desire for a high destiny with God. It dissuaded him from murder, and gained a marriage to a godly king for her!

When it comes to the topic of submission, most every woman thinks she is an unusual case, that her personality has inordinate trouble getting itself in line in this area. She is convinced that submission is extra hard for her especially. The truth is, all women have this struggle. They just are unaware that others have the same trouble because they haven't interviewed enough of them! You are not an exceptional case or somehow a woman that God can't handle or has separate instructions for. There is blessing in obeying one's husband in all matters where we can.

If we really are bent on throwing out the entire concept of submission in the marriage context, then the next logical step is for a woman to avoid taking the man's last name when she marries, and to avoid moving where his job would indicate. She may find that she prefers to have them both live in two different cities to accommodate both jobs, shuffling the children in between for years on end. Or for that matter, she may prefer never to marry, really. Use the guy. Dump the vow. It is not surprising to note that all of these deviances are now cultural norms. We were only too ready to adopt them as a direct result of this foundational departure from the Biblical understanding of the institution and structure of marriage. It has not resulted in a better world. Now over 40% of children are born out of wedlock, and over 50% of marriageable people don't even *believe* in marriage anymore. The preference for living together has really been traded for spiritually dying together. Civilization as we have known it is gone.

Roles

A companion hot button for our culture is the issue of assumed Biblical roles in marriage. The culture hates the pictures of a woman with an apron and a spoon and a man tinkering with the mechanics of his car so much that they have virtually taken all such pictures out of the school textbooks and much of the juvenile sections of libraries. There are loud protests that men should do women's work as housedads and vice versa. This discussion has become so heated that it has reached absurd proportions in universities.

One man spoke about a woman's studies course he was required to take, because the administration knew he was so conservative they were afraid to have him graduate with *their* school's name attached to him. They tried one last ditch effort to get him to liberalize by requiring that he take a women's studies course to "round out his education." He was the only *guy* in the class. In that class, during one session, half the women yelled loudly that it was unfair that women are tied down to nursing babies and suggested that we needed to work on a way to get men biologically fixed with breasts so that they too could nurse! Meanwhile, the other half yelled that it would be giving the men too much control/power in the home! The fellow picked his way through the course's landmines, and after graduation continued in his Biblical persuasions. Jettisoning any belief in the entire course's contents, he married and fathered eight very stable children, leading a very *happy* home. One has only to guess what the homes of the raging women in that class look like, 20 years later.

Fight it as we might, Biblical roles for men and women have stood the test of time and the test of biology. They simply WORK better. Understanding them and living in the light of them produces unparalleled order and well-being in the home. Beginning a home with a lack of this basic understanding of roles has left every piece of the domestic work-load up for grabs. Household after household has descended into chaos, with irritations galore, and severe depressions over dashed expectations. Countless young homes are a free-for-all every day of the week. The sparks fly; disorder rules the day and the night.

Every man and every woman *can* exchange roles and *do* exchange roles, either during times of emergencies (a man may temporarily cook for his wife while his wife has a baby) or as gifts of love (when a woman temporarily changes the tires on the bikes while her husband's back is out). But exchanging roles is more *taxing* on each spouse. The roles are more easily done by the appropriate gender. After all, biology does indicate a companion psychology. To say that biology does *not* indicate some degree of who we are in essence would be as absurd as saying that all owls have been given lizard's brains—whatever FOR? Men have large muscles for a *reason*: to wield the hammer. Women have breasts for a *reason*: they are going to need them. Yes, some man and some woman may end up doing the job or carrying the role of the opposite gender, and some may do this for long seasons, seemingly quite successfully, but sooner or later they will wear out. It will tax them more to do what they were not psychologically or biologically intended to do than to do what they were *primarily* designed to do. Substantial stress will accrue over the long haul. A bird *can* drag dead cats up a hill, to loud applause for doing so, but at some point he will wear out. He was meant to fly. Dogs drag dead cats up hills quite easily.

FERTILIZE

9

EXPECTATIONS AND YARDSTICKS

Having respect for our spouse's totally different wiring means we drop the yardsticks. Subconsciously we each have different yardsticks by which we measure each other. One spouse's yardstick might be filled with inches marked "punctuality and properness"; another's might be marked "wanderlust and exploration"; another's, "industry/production." Each person's yardstick is different. One spouse wants to spend money for broadening family experiences now; the other wants to save for a secure fiscal future. While we hold our yardstick up to our husband we are, at first, unaware that he simultaneously holds quite a different yardstick up to us. Sadly, try as we may, we all fall short of each other's measurements. How much more peaceful it is to throw the yardsticks away.

It is simply unfair to require of a mate to be both ends of even his own yardstick. If a person is a perfectionist, it is wrong of us to expect him to be functioning loosely and quickly at the other end of that yardstick. If he is a good listener, he is probably not going to also be an articulate life-of-the-party talker. If he is good at details he probably is not also good at getting "the big picture." If he is a visionary, details will fall through the cracks by the thousands; you can count on it.

All of us carry "expectation software" inside of us. It is written there without our ever knowing it, influenced by stories all the way from *Sleeping Beauty* to romance books and observing only the dress parade of other marriages. Movies create a lot of this baggage. They condense life into mere snap-shots, turn-of-event moments, in optimal settings, that no real life could ever measure up to. But we tell ourselves it is supposed to—hence the birth of deep disappointment.

In his book *Life Together*, Dietrich Bonhoeffer states that every community—whether it be church, 4-H, or marriage—must go through a process of crashing and dying first in order to begin building real God-like life. The quicker you can die to "the way it should be" and making comparisons with friend's marriages, the better.

Not only do we arrive at marriage with expecta-tions, there also are new expectations that we raise for each other *after* marriage. "You said you'd be home at five o'clock." "Why aren't the dishes done?" We find ourselves tying each other up like marital Lazaruses.

The deep down wonderful secret to happiness is to **expect nothing**! Then everything nice that does happen is gravy. If you view life as a temporary boot-camp, it's not too bad; if you were expecting heaven, it's awful. It's all a question of perspective.

Consider what would make you happy in a prison cell. You'd be so grateful just to have a rickety old wooden chair so that your legs wouldn't cramp from sitting on the floor. So if that is the only furniture you have in your fine three-bedroom home, be grateful that you have the chair *and* space. If your husband speaks crossly to you, you *can* overlook it and be grateful that you even *have* a husband!

After a lifetime of brilliantly observing life as it really is, the acclaimed British editorialist G. K. Chesterton wrote about the universal tendencies of both men and women within marriage: "Women view men as hopelessly self-centered; men view women as chronically cross." Whew. After initially arguing with myself against the idea that I was cross, I watched more closely and found it to be true of me far too often! *Expect* your husband to be self-centered, and get on with it.

Most of us fall into the trap of defining our whole marriage by the one cantankerous moment we're now in. If your husband is being really ugly to you, you might tend to feel that "he's just a beast." But keep in mind that your beast is also paying the bills, going to church, fixing things, and not having an affair! Don't expect him to be anything other than a beast and you'll be happy at the "oh so many moments of unexpected kindness!" Having no expectations is positively freeing. Remind yourself that your husband is a larger person than that one irritating quality that is in front of you right now.

If you expect that your marriage is built on mutual compromises, consciously working out one sore spot after another, you may be disappointed. When I was first married, a wise older woman told me it is easier to save your breath and just adapt. Yes, adapt, adapt, adapt when it comes to these thousand little inconveniences, slights and selfishnesses. Downright blindness is a good way to go. Most marital conflict is of this sort rather than of raw moral dilemma. Work at adapting to what *is*, rather than aiming at some notion of an ideal lifestyle with the ideal husband. Size up the landscape and figure out some way to cope. If he's chronically late for dinner, serve him cheerfully when he *does* come home, rather than arresting him at the door with a barrage of expectations that only bring relational death.

Can all expectations be worked out? No. In some areas you'll just flat go to the grave with different views. But relax! It's possible to hold greatly different opinions and still get along. Some areas may need to be confronted eventually but can wait, even years, while other areas need tending to now. Building a marriage is not at all like building a house, where every corner must be shaved precisely to keep it from falling down. Marriage is more like going sailing, tilting the sail this way and that to catch the favorable winds as you go.

My wise father's statement that "Marriage is an adventure in adjustment," is true. Adventure—because no one has ever been through your particular duo-dynamic before. It is uncharted waters. In the beginning marriage is much like the grand junction of two roaring rivers colliding and crashing at the meeting place but which will eventually run calmly together somewhere downstream. Adjustment? Like a fine clock maker who constantly tinkers to "make it better," you'll find that you increasingly refine your responses to your mate over time.

You cannot change another person. So you can let go of that expectation. There is too much history before your mate ever gets to you. *Any* adult has a psyche that has developed, along with interests, propensities, giftings, passions, ambitions, habits and weaknesses that are already heavily imprinted. We all carry with us personal modus operandi developed far beyond pliability. A mate comes to you, and you come to him, already hard-wired. A spouse simply is not going to have success remaking their mate. There will be some gentle influence upon each other, like the sun warming the crust of the earth, but the basic material has already been laid down deep. Your husband's deeper self will rearrange itself but it will be under God's sure guiding hand alone, and only in God's timing.

In the meantime, instead of viewing your man's wiring as something to endure or put up with, shift gears and learn to actually appreciate it and even marvel at it. It has been said, "Where good men differ, walk softly," and never is that more true than in marriage. We come into marriage bent on remaking each other like bulls in a china closet, but over time, we learn to walk softly.

C. S. Lewis said that one of his chief joys in marriage was discovering "otherness." It is a relief from self. Hell is unmitigated self: self, ad nauseam. If understood and entered into rightly, a marriage relationship can become an earlier heaven. Heaven is all about *relationships*, first with the Creator and then with each other. That agenda angers the

Enemy. Busting up the earthly paradise of blissful relationships is the Enemy's main goal. That is why marriage is constantly in derision. The Enemy blocks the process of relational advancement at every turn, on purpose. "We wrestle not against flesh and blood" (Ephesians 6:12 KJV).

Just as we can't change our mate, we don't/can't make marital oneness, either. Scripture puts it this way in Matthew 19:5: "The two shall become one." It is something that God does to us over a lifetime of relating. He does it so well that some elderly couples even start looking like each other! Oneness is not achieved by holding each other under a magnifying glass.

Not trusting God to change your husband is in essence saying, "There is no God for me in this matter" (à la Psalm 14:1 and 53:1). Trying to control your husband often puts a wedge between your husband and the direct convicting power of the Holy Spirit. It needlessly exhausts you and can block God's own pressure upon your husband. Watch God change him through prayer alone (as He also changes you). God will do a far better job of it than you could.

And what of our expectations for romance? The devastating effect of reading romance novels and watching romantic movies is that it sets up a frustration of looking for romance to be expressed in marriage in certain specific ways. Most men don't even know a woman *has* these expectations, let alone know how to meet them. This dive-bombs the marriage from day one. The wife begins on the wrong footing. Gaping loneliness, dashed expectations and bitterness waste years before the aging bride wakes up to what actually exists.

In contrast to the straightforwardness of the man, a woman is complex. Complexity was given to her by God, not for endless romantic escapades but to serve her man. Not so that she could demand that the man would meet her psychological needs at every point—as we've been erroneously taught by the women's feminist movement—but so that this complexity would give her an infinite capacity to adjust and adapt to her husband! She needs this complexity to relate deeply and sensitively with each of their growing children, too, and to carry on multiple domestic tasks at one time without going crazy. So, the point is not to expect our husbands to fulfill *us*, but to put our capacity for complexity to use to serve him.

Expectations kill relationships. Expectations are equivalent to putting a straightjacket on your mate. Instead of getting the change you desired in him, you'll wind up dealing with the dust of his many and varied excuses and escapes.

Conversely, appreciation causes a relationship to flourish. Nobody blossoms under "shoulds" and "oughts" and "naughty-naughties" and "never-arrivings" and "never-enoughs," and "chronic disgruntlements," and "micro-managings" and "macro-maneuverings." These all feel like a blade to your mate, and he will increasingly desire to avoid passing near you because it cuts and nicks his spirit. Conversely, a loved mate will go to great lengths to be with you and stay with you at every chance, when you make him feel good psychologically.

Give each other space to be who you/they are without chronic censoriousness. Major on encouragement and goodwill. Refrain from carving on each other to make your mate into an image of yourself. Remember that marriage is optimally a departure from "self"; it is an enrichment of each other's lives, and a way of seeing life through two sets of lenses. Marriage puts a boundary on unbridled "me-ism." It forms a protection from narrow-mindedness. Marriage exemplifies synergism. In other words, 2 + 2 does not equal 4 in marriage; it equals 9 or 56. Learning to cooperate with the design of marriage transforms you over time into more than what you were before.

Lower your expectations for what the marriage will give you. If you have a difficult marriage, saying, "This is my lot," can take the edge off. Treasure the times you have with affirming friends and relatives, and continue to demonstrate Christ's enduring love to your husband. All of what you experience will eventually sanctify you. Much heart rest can result from meditating upon the following scriptures: Philippians 2:3-4, Romans 15:7, Proverbs 20:3 and 22, James 4:6-7, and 2 Corinthians 3:18.

Because we are all imperfect beings, change is needed in all of us. Our gut-wrenching joint practical decisions in marriage always could be wiser, and the holiness quotient in our homes could be improved. But the question is, how do we get there? God gets us there. The *pace* at which God effects these changes is His alone to mastermind. At the end of life, we may be surprised to find that the improvement of our mate may not even be the primary agenda of marriage—growing a seasoned mercy in our own hearts might be.

Since we *can* change only ourselves for the

better, why not turn our attention there? Why not get busy with that project? What if we quietly worked on a hidden agenda to improve *ourselves*? That's daunting, perhaps, but not impossible. Enjoyable, even? Could it become a contest that puts some zing back into our life? Improve our own productivity. Upgrade and polish our domestic skills. Become really good at the various aspects of homemaking and other skills. Get busy educating and refining our children. Strive to give up small mannerisms that we know that our mate finds irritating, making ourselves as pleasant to be around as possible. As a by-product of our new focus of aggressively going after improving ourselves, a strange happiness can begin to creep over us!

Expectations mess with our heads and destroy our chances for real joy with what *is*. Rigid things get broken. Our earthly happiness hinges on our ability to make lemonade out of lemons—to find the possibilities in what already exists. When we make our peace with the knowledge that all of our present circumstances and all of our relationships are sovereignly from His hand, it promotes emotional well-being. God is working out great and lofty purposes through our marriage, which we know not yet. But we *will* know *then*. "The will of the LORD is good, acceptable, and perfect" (Romans 12:2).

10

COMMUNICATION OR MENTAL TELEPATHY

Communication within marriage is not about winning and losing. Yet there is some cursed tendency in all of us to verbally want to "duke it out" until the other person is reduced to a pulp and we win. To have a good marriage, we must work at halting this tendency in ourselves. Any communication within marriage has to be all about enlargement for both people. Think about it this way: if one of you wins, your marriage might be lost. Instead, fight to keep the *marriage* winning. The old adage, "You can win the battle but lose the war," applies to any marital argument. The sinful nature in each of us wants to win at any price. But in marriage the price may be too high. Remind yourself frequently that your spouse is not your enemy, the Devil is.

If communication only resembles a boxing ring, it results in battered and bruised and knocked out individuals. Communication is about promoting understanding and heightening awareness, not about dueling.

So, the first rule of good communication is to express the value of your husband and marriage at the beginning, middle and end of conflict.

Stuffing communication in a marriage doesn't work. Although you succeed in guarding your tongue, your body language is communicating something different. Your emotional distance is communicating, your face is communicating, your silence is communicating, and your lack of cooperation is communicating. The way you feel about things will come out, one way or the other.

Remember that marital conflict is not all bad. Sometimes relationships gain higher ground via working through some rough patches. Have the courage to communicate verbally. Your husband can't read your mind. If he is going to understand you and you him, you have to overcome your own inertia and try to communicate. This takes courage when difficult hours come. It is far easier to stuff agitations and explode later. It's true that the difficult hour is not the time to discuss it, but it's important to bring the problem back up sometime soon. Resolving issues in a timely way, as soon as is *calmly* possible, keeps the relationship healthy, free of bitterness. The Bible only allows for one day. While you're brooding, the sun is sinking! (See Ephesians 4:26.)

Sometimes, sufficient emotional combustion is needed to get the issue out of grey fog into actual articulation, when lack of courage at other times has stuffed it. Combustion overwhelms our lethargy to communicate when we had thought it would be too much work. But when those moments arrive, it is our manner of expressing ourselves that is critical.

Communication must eventually leave the parameters of venting and get to the vast acreage of building, restoring, and caring.

To combine honesty in communication with the habit of subduing yourself takes some recalibration of habits, and increased "on-the-spot" prayers. If you grow angry, take a walk and pray for a calm mind and a godly attitude to help you return to having a holy response ("Be ye holy as I am holy" 1 Peter 1:16). And then try picturing yourself as a resilient stable punching bag! Recall how each time it is hit, it swings back to a straight position. The law of gravity supersedes the punching bag's responsiveness to the hits. And so it is to be with you. The law of love calls you back from your legitimate responses that lay you low and hurt. The heart of every couple has to return to an upright position, not once but over and over again.

Communicate honestly—express your wishes or desires; share insights, forebodings, and fears—and then quickly resume the posture of cheerful contentment.

How you communicate and *when* you communicate can make or break a marriage. In general, the rule of thumb is to keep communication short at the time of crisis (for example, "That hurts" or "I don't feel comfortable with this") and simply remain quiet and figure out some way to navigate through the disaster with the minimum amount of relational/circumstantial damage at the moment. Put the best face on everything, at the time. Then *later*, discuss the destructive dynamic at a calm moment. Set aside a time when the children are not around. Little tummies cannot bear adult conflict. Discuss it, and then fully forgive one another. Dregs of leftover unforgiveness leave ash in the stomach; this is often true, not only figuratively but also literally, as health breaks down.

Sandwich your statements about hope for change between statements about what is already good. Knowing that as a wife you have much need of sanctification, too, triple-star this in your thinking: **it is not *what* you say, but the *manner* in which you say it** that builds or destroys a marriage.

Communication necessitates ongoing *effort* to function well as a twosome. It means you have to slow down a bit in making some larger decisions from the way you did it when you were single. Communication takes time. Ideas have to be worked through *two* heads now. That process has its wonderful advantages. Although it can feel inhibiting at times, it was really designed for our safety, even morally. Knowing that our thought processes are being observed has a curbing effect upon our irresponsibilities and subtle evil inclinations. And having to communicate about so many things requires a wonderful fellowship *as we live*. That is difficult for us, living in a culture that is dominated by speed and efficiency. Having to eat together three times a day, too, looks suspiciously like it was divinely engineered that way, to make sure fellowship happens with one's mate.

You simply must make the effort to communicate about tensions and reoccurring problems. You can't expect your spouse to always be reading your mind, or expect that somehow "he should just know." Don't cast up your arms and say, "What's the use?" The "use" is the preservation of your marriage.

Part of being a helpmate is adding perception—but with a loose hand. If after clearly seeing your point of view, he opts for a different course, he is in God's hand, still. It is then that God's good gift of submission comes into play, for the wife.

However, even as you seek to improve your communication it is helpful to remember that communication is not the fixer-upper for everything. It is not as powerful and effective as prayer. In fact, some areas won't respond at all to communication—if your spouse is trapped in some addiction, for example.

In most cases, though, good communication will accomplish a great deal toward ending conflict. That is to say, good mature communication does. My husband and I recently asked an elderly married couple what was the secret of their 50-year marriage. They both immediately piped up: communication. The elderly lady followed with, "In the early days of our marriage, I communicated all right. I communicated with my body and a scowl on my face!"

During the week, most married folks' conversations plateau to a merely functional level. "Did you pay the bills?" "What do you want to eat?" "Did Jamie's shoes got cleaned up yet?" To communicate about deeper things requires some extra thought and effort and time.

To keep the communication process moving along at significant levels, a helpful habit is to evaluate the week in writing in four areas and then share these areas with each other. If you want to do this, divide a sheet of paper into four sections:

accomplishments, memories, frustrations, and new directions. You might find yourselves saying, during this process, "Oh, I didn't know that meant so much to you!" or "You were bothered by that? That's easy to fix."

You need each other's input. You will see things he doesn't see, and vice versa. You are one, but each of you is a very different perceiver. Consider your own face for a moment. You have two eyes, two ears, two nostrils, all giving sensory input to your brain—but only one mouth to say what you are actually going to do. The face is a beautiful picture of how the man and woman can operate together. You both give input, but in the end the husband is the mouthpiece, the one responsible to chart the family's course if there is an impasse. It is impossible to walk in two directions at once. But generally most issues don't become an either/or case. Through discussion, the right direction often becomes apparent to both, resulting in unity in *most* decisions.

To stuff your frustrations robs your spouse of vital input. So, make sure your communication is open, sharing as you go. Try to bring one another along in your *temporary* thinking so that you don't startle one another with your *finished* thoughts.

Here is an example. Suppose a woman has been thinking for some time that the family needs a lamp with a swing arm to read better by. In the evenings she often observes that the children are squinting when they read. She grows in her conviction that they should do it as soon as possible. The next time they are near a lamp store she suddenly says, "I want to go in and buy a lamp." Explosion. Husband says,

"We don't need a lamp!" Because she hasn't brought him along in her thinking, he thinks her request is absurd. She thinks he is highly unreasonable and they both walk away frustrated with one another. You need to share your thinking as it develops all along the way. If the husband had had more time to think about the lamp he could have been drawn to observe the children squinting, too, and in the end even found one on sale at a better price. Any topic would fit this scenario with the same results. Perhaps one spouse wants two vacations a year and the other wants to go to more baseball games. You need to share your thinking as it develops all along for an easier go at mutual understanding over all issues.

The secret to being a vessel of godly input is to hold oneself back from demanding change on the basis of that input. The nagging wife is the wife who demands change. The husband will stiffen his neck and harden his heart if he feels run by the woman. After giving honest input, it is then our job to back off and entrust the area to God. It is all right to give the same input as different situations arise that verify the point, but the husband must feel free to make his own decisions.

So, don't hold your husband to the flame, demanding instant conversions of habit. Doing this in a discussion causes an arena of understanding to quickly turn into an arena of control. Most men think seriously about a wife's input over some time, even if they don't seem to at the moment. Often men will change their behavior in the future, even though they say nothing about it at the time when the matter is brought to their attention. Your job is to communicate what you feel. How he responds is his own matter of his internal counsel.

After discussions of deeply difficult issues, your husband may seem overwhelmed or seem withdrawn, so create a cheerful, hopeful atmosphere and manifest goodwill to help your husband find his way back to you. Do not hold your husband under a lingering disapproval, if you have had any. Some women tyrannize their husbands with the silent treatment. Nowhere is this attitude authorized in the Bible or seen in the nature of Christ, who never withdraws from us, even when chastening us. Give him a bridge. Do some specific good deed to your husband—something tangible that communicates kindness.

It is important to note that long conversations are not the only way to communicate. Sometimes short sentences are more effective. You do not have to lock horns over every small issue. The same thing can be communicated on the backstroke with far less taxation to you both. "Honey, perhaps that comment might hurt your son; you might want to re-examine it?" Then change the conversation. Move on. Posturing statements in the form of a question can leave a spouse with more dignity, too.

It is the tribunal, the instant courtroom, the amassing of judge and jury and time, that frustrates a husband in dealing with conflict. Sometimes such kinds of efforts are necessary when the issues are severe, but in general the same thing can often be accomplished by sharing a respectful "awareness" comment and get past it. Water your garden with refreshing gentle rains, not hailstorms. Not many things grow well in high velocity wind.

A woman is not meant to fight with a man; it will wear her out. In a marital fight a man *can't* back down; he is built to win, to compete, to conquer. Fighting will get you nowhere. Ranting and raving and crying over an issue won't change your husband one iota. A man doesn't know what to do with tears.

But the power of a deferring spirit, reverent respectful language, and appealing to his authority— now that kind of relating has a different *feel.* Presenting this kind of demeanor diffuses the tension—this isn't anything he needs to conquer. He has room to ruminate on your idea; he has space to consider its validity.

After God showed me this, one time I went to my husband and said, "Honey, I don't want to harangue you over this repeating issue, so the next time it happens and I become frustrated, what should I do?" Seeing my broken spirit, he told me to write him a note in the midst of it saying that it was happening again—and to leave the results with him. The next time he observed my servant heart in letting him know, in a note, he stopped the frustrating circumstance immediately.

It is chaste behavior and not railing that will win our husbands. Truly the verse in 1 Peter 3 is packed with wisdom from above. Husbands will be won by our behavior, even more than by our words.

Just a quick aside here. If you are prone to excessive anger, check your monthly cycle by your calendar. It may be sheer chemistry that is defeating you. If you know you are coming up on ovulation or the end of your monthly cycle, decide ahead of time to avoid conflict during those times, writing "be careful" over those days on the calendar! Save the issue for later. Put yourself under extra self-control during those days so that you don't regret your own outbursts.

Often, simple good verbal communication can clear up differences within a matter of minutes. Try to keep the tensions diffused as new problems emerge. If an issue crops up over dinner, for example, both of you can leave the table, go someplace where you can communicate quickly in private, resolve it, and come back with an unclouded countenance and a loving heart toward one another.

On the other hand, resolving more complex conflicts will need time and paper. It helps to see some issues in black and white. One time my husband and I were chafing under several days of hit-and-run remarks over what to do with a lump of savings we had accrued, given our present circumstances and needs. Finally, I suggested that we look at our differences on paper. I asked him to tell me what he would do with the money if I were out of the picture. Then I told him what I'd do if he were not here. We saw that these two viewpoints were poles apart, so I put them on opposite sides of the paper. We then started working toward center. We both shared our reasons candidly and freely, since this was all just "hypothetical on paper." The problem solved itself as we saw how we could modify our individual goals to reach a mutual goal that would benefit both of us *more* than our individual goals. By viewing the dilemma as ideas on paper rather than as a boxing match that one of us would win or lose, we were freed up to see objectively what had to be done.

To cope with your spouse's irritating qualities that don't get modified or removed even after repeated attempts at communication, just mentally check out over those issues. Stay relationally warm toward him, but create a happy life for yourself. Don't ride his ups and downs. You only get one life to live. It seems smartest to figure out how to survive as pleasantly as possible. A tent can become a palace if you'll merely entertain the idea mentally and fan *that* flame. The placement of your mind makes all the difference.

With some marital problems we may find ourselves permanently on the shores of perplexity. A spouse might not be able to get past something psychologically, even just within himself. To continue to exert effort to change areas in your man that have been met with again and again with no change or understanding might not be beneficial to either of you. It could be like telling a stutterer to "stop stuttering" or a crippled person to "just walk!" There can be impediments in the mind or emotion or spirit of a person that are every bit as real as a physical malady. You may have such a place in you, too. Real love looks past the inability. Just picture your mate in a wheelchair, instead of his having a mental block, and you'll wonderfully find yourself modifying your responses next time.

A godly old man who was a pastor and full of wise counsel suggested that a married couple not take everything to the mat (as wrestlers do). He noted that many happier couples have learned to just let some stuff go. Every situation in life doesn't need human rectification, nor must we persuade everyone of our point of view. We were not ultimately called to be each other's governors, but each other's lovers. God is far more anxious for our spouse's sanctification than we are. We'll find liberating heart rest by depositing many of our disputes on the banks of the river of prayer. A person would rather relate to a gentle companion all day long than a lawyer. You will find your spouse far more amiable when he is not brought to task about his every action.

Communicating without words

There is much good influence that a wife can quietly exert over a man by exposing him to wholesome materials. First-rate books, uplifting company/visitors, inspiring stories related over the dinner table, bringing home or ordering teaching CDs and DVDs, going to seminars, workshops and conventions (all for the increase of holy living between you), can have a wonderful effect upon your man without his having to hear it from your lips. You can set such materials around the house, hand them to him, recommend them to him, or even ask in such an open manner as, "Honey, are you comfortable with where we are financially, or would you like a book on money that I heard was really good on this radio show, that is helping a lot of people get out of debt? I'd be happy to get it for you if you would like it. But I won't bother pursuing it if you are not interested at this point."

Perhaps the best form of communication with a man has nothing to do with talk, at all, but has to do with sometimes choosing to just be quietly near him, side by side, as he works. Just your silent focused attention upon him gladdens a man's heart and refreshes him as few other forms of relating do. Companionship of this sort builds up your man. A man's delight may not be in the foo-foo of candle-light dinners, presents, and elaborate surprise parties, that so many women *think* will improve things (actually to delight themselves), but rather in quiet affirmation, choosing to be there for him above all others.

WEEDING

11

STEPS TO CONFLICT RESOLUTION

Before we learn some ways to resolve conflict, let's ask the question: is it even possible to resolve conflict on all fronts with a spouse? With even a cursory look, it appears not. There are problems in almost every marriage that will not be resolved this side of the grave. Make your peace with the fact that complete resolution is not the aim of marriage; loving well in spite of the complexity is.

Secondly, let's get comfortable with the idea that conflict is not necessarily bad. Sometimes relationships have to go *through* something to get them to a better place. Sometimes conflict is the *only* pathway to better understandings and smoother sailing. Do not shrink back from the process, if it is needed. Do not *fear* conflict. Toughen up emotionally, to face your particular and specific realities maturely and to *do* something about them. Conflict resolution is a major part of all marriages. It comes as a surprise to newlyweds, but for all married people, over time, it is the grist of becoming larger people. The phrase: "I don't quite see it like that, could we discuss it further?" opens up worlds of insights for *both* partners. It is a gentle and non-threatening way to enlarge the horizons. Diffusing the threat of communication, lowering the tensions, and coming to see communication as a *benefit* to you both is where you are headed. Communication is an adventure in bigger understandings.

Yelling indicates panic, that there isn't enough time to hear both sides. Yelling indicates that one side or the other feels threatened or is on the verge of feeling annihilated, just for having feelings and thoughts. Some spouses don't *want* increased understandings but *only* want to get their own way, stubbornly unaware that an even *better* solution may be on the horizon. These have to be gently shown in many cases how it is to *their* advantage to talk a little more or to go for more counsel. When one spouse feels like they are withering while the other spouse is winning, that is not the kind of an atmosphere where understanding is enhanced. We've got to get outside the boxing ring into the phone booth with our communications, actually *wanting* more communication! Two sets of eyes, ears and brains just may produce *better* outcomes every time!

However, don't wait to get all of the conflicts out of your marriage before you find some large purpose to live for *together*. Such an hour would never come. A big joint purpose will help get your sights up and out of yourselves, and off from endless marital introspection. Despite our best efforts we won't improve much, so hurling energy at doing some good in the world is a far better obsession than re-doing each other. Raising children will be the first of those life-giving "beyond ourselves external" obsessions!

If you don't have a strong relational life within your core relationship of marriage, you're dead in the water. If you want spiritual power in your life, let other relationships suffer, if need be, but not that one. You are never more of a person than what your spouse experiences of you in your own home. Only he knows what you are when you are not out on dress parade living before a vast sea of faces in the big wide world. The home is the place to do our *homework* in growing up relationally and maturing ourselves as individuals.

We all know how to relate at home when things are going well. It's when things go south that we have a hard time. No matter how finessed a person is at avoiding interpersonal land mines, it's impossible to avoid all of a family's relational colliding. Because we all are human and have a fallen nature, tough relational patches are a part of life. The marital fray can get exceptionally messy in an hour when all of our "old men" bump into one another, simultaneously! However, as Believers, each of us contains a "new man" to trump that "old man" (2 Corinthians 5:17, Galatians 6:15). It's how we respond as the new man in our thought life *afterwards* that matters. That's why David said, "May the words of my mouth and the meditations of my heart be acceptable unto you, oh LORD" (Psalm 19:14). Our aim is to think thoughts after God, immediately after we catch ourselves having had our own ugly thoughts.

In your thought life, make those meditations of your heart be right. Moment by moment, fix them, mend them, build them, and patch them until they hold up under the Heavenly Father's scrutiny. The most powerful way to arrest wayward meditations is to lasso them with Scripture. Have several verses handy for your mind to grab when needed.

We must leave no destructive thought unchallenged by the good. As C. S. Lewis said: "Every inch of the universe has been claimed and counterclaimed." Furthermore, no thought is ever static; it *leads* somewhere.

How to approach conflict resolution

First: pray for your husband. On days when he may have a headache, a hidden anxiety, or a knee-jerk response from childhood, prayer will immediately change him (in your own mind) from your bitter enemy (at the moment) to your needy brother. Prayer is the primary way in which you are your husband's helpmeet. You have an "in" with God for him because he is your husband, and because no one in the entire world will ever pray for him as passionately as you will.

If your husband is stumbling, it may be because you haven't given him enough prayer cover. When we quarrel and fight, all we can see are our rights. The minute we stop and begin to pray, we get objectivity on our husbands. You will simply be amazed at the objectivity and depth of insight you'll have about your husband when you begin to seriously, daily pray for him. You'll find that as you pray God will give you additional unique, specific wisdom in how to relate to him, as only you can do. Love for him rushes into your soul as you see him as God sees him. You will see root causes behind present behaviors, and mercy for him will spill all over your heart. Sadly, we tend to pray for family, friends, missionaries, neighbors and others more than for our own husbands. Cover him with lots of prayer.

If there is a moment when your other half has been harsh, cranky, critical, or impatient, Satan may fling a thought into your mind, "Some other man might be better." He would *not.* "All have sinned and fallen short of the glory of God," including the next guy. It is a delusion that some other man would have been better.

If your spouse becomes totally irksome and un-reasonable, you can say to yourself, "Well, someone has got to love him at this hour. In such a mood he would drive everyone *else* away! I'll stick with him over this rocky ground to stabilize him and help get him back on track." By deliberately operating in the opposite spirit, doing something extra nice, you can often break up the fallow ground. Just plow right over it with love.

Take his moments of contrariness as an exciting challenge. Privately asking yourself, "How will I do, *this* time?" Learn to view his off moments as char-acter growth boot camp for you. A woman's flexi-bility, ingenuity and intuition especially fit her for just such a purpose.

If your husband shirks certain duties in one area or another, saddle up next to him and actually help him finish the task. He may just be paralyzed by the thought of it and needs a buddy. Try tackling the unwanted project together. There are *reasons* why a spouse is resistant to certain tasks. If punctuality or procrastination is his problem, (and you happen to be strong in those areas) show him the advantage to *himself* of starting earlier next time, by letting him experience it a time or two *with* you. Initially get "in" the solution for your husband. A helpmeet *helps!*

If you are prone to anger, learn how to wrench your thoughts away from the present exasperating moment and fixate on a totally different idea, a pleasant project you're working on, a pleasant person you know, or a piece of beauty you like to see. The moment will pass, you'll have no regrets, and you can take up discussion of it at a time that is less volatile for both of you. Train yourself to immediately look to the LORD when you're about to lose it. It's a mystery; it's a miracle on command, at your disposal, at any time, anywhere. Use it. Anger is not an attribute of the wise, as Proverbs states: "A fool gives full vent to his anger, but a wise man keeps himself under control" (Proverbs 29:11).

Be swift to forgive. As one Christian martyr wrote, "Don't waste your vital strength on unforgiveness toward your torturer." *Get over it* and *get on with it.*

God has given you special grace for your particular man. There are irritating qualities about your husband that would drive another woman crazy. She simply doesn't have the grace for them. Conversely, there are things about her husband that would drive *you* crazy. You don't have the grace for *her* husband.

Let me give you a fun example. One day one of my husband's ex-roommates came to visit us. My husband was tied up in a meeting so this friend took me for a drive. He wanted me to show him the campus while we waited, but he would do the driving. This guy drove so slowly, it nearly drove me crazy!

My husband drives decisively and purposefully. I had to bite my tongue to keep from saying, "Come on, move it."

Conversely a friend of mine, when traveling with us, catches her breath that my husband eats and drives at the same time, and shaves and reads maps, and, and, and ... "What is your all-fired hurry?" she complains. "Isn't there even time to stop, go in, sit down, and enjoy a meal?"

You have a special grace to match all of your husband's idiosyncrasies, and only you have it. Bill Gothard said once, "Never take up someone else's offense, because you won't have the grace for it." God immediately gives the wounded person the grace to forgive. But He doesn't give that same grace to that person's friends and relatives. For example, I had a friend who in a moment of anger told her parents of a hurtful thing her husband did. She got over it long before her parents did. She forgave and forgot, but her parents still harbored it months later.

Every marriage has not only these small idiosyncrasies but big problems as well. God has given you special grace to handle the specific kind in your own marriage. It is comforting to know that God is lovingly sovereign in picking you exclusively to live with those particular challenges. He matched your character need with your husband's weaknesses.

If we can see our problems as something God allows for our maximum character development rather than as mistakes we fell into that we must desperately find a way out of, we'll have much more peace in our life together.

It is within marriage that we'll experience our greatest failure. God uses marriage to bring us into wholehearted agreement that we are sinners in need of a Savior—something He knew all along. Marriage is often the arena where we come to the end of ourselves. It forces us into the supernatural to drink gustily of its powers of love. As the old hymn says: "When we have exhausted our hoarded resources, our Father's full giving has only begun."

Conflict resolution tactics

For those many marital moments when we feel like we bang into the same domestic problems over and over and never reach a solution, here are some specific helps to isolate a problem and work it totally through. Most marriages have some problems that have never been resolved, that *can* be resolved with a little "know how". These are issues where spouses may have resorted to silence because it's just too draining to bring them up again? Here is a way to quickly reach some satisfying resolutions to these fixable problems —without the battle scars.

Vent on paper. Let what you write be filled with "I feel" statements rather than "You do" statements. Refrain from out-of-control language. Resorting to your own wicked expressions is not an appropriate vehicle for expressing frustration. When finished venting with the pencil, try to summarize the *core* issue at stake in two or three succinct sentences. That final summary is marital communication gold. Those few sentences become something that your spouse can deal with positively, should you choose to share them with him. Just this general writing exercise, alone, can stimulate good conversation and solve many problems. But if you need a more detailed step by step approach, it follows. Take your core issues, one by one and follow these progressive steps and you'll come out on higher ground, while suffering less trauma to get there!

The six steps to resolution

1. <u>Isolate a single problem</u> (be very specific and limited) and focus only on it. Writing it out avoids the verbal spray or unloading syndrome—hit-and-run behavior, grandiose generalizing, or "you-always" approach to venting with each other that:

- Feels like a relief to the one doing it, but
- Overwhelms the other person with awful feelings and is unfair, and
- Doesn't bring even one point to complete, satisfying resolution for both parties.

Note: The first area of conflict you choose to write out should be one you don't care too much about, but one that's a source of some irritation between you. That way, you can focus on learning the procedure without worrying about the results.

Usually the wife writes out steps 1-4; we've found that generally most men don't have the patience for it. However, the man comments upon or writes out the shorter, concise finished solution in step 5.

2. <u>Write the problem as you see it</u>—from your point of view. This allows you to vent, to say everything you've been stuffing, without feeling like you're being interrupted or railroaded or dominated by your husband. Couch your own anxieties amidst statements like: "I know you didn't mean this, you

probably didn't see this part of it, I know you meant no harm."

3. <u>Write the same problem from the way you think your husband sees it.</u> This step forces you to see things from his point of view. After fully getting into his mindset, you may find yourself actually crumbling up your paper because the problem has ceased to be important to you now that you have thought about it from his perspective. In addition, seeing the issue from his point of view may suggest a resolution that you hadn't thought of before.

4. <u>Write out an ideal solution for you and for your husband</u>—the solution that you think will truly iron out the problem. "As I see it, it would be far more efficient if we proceeded this way, but what do *you* think!?"

5. <u>Share each of these four steps with your husband</u>—at a calm time, not when you're in the heat of battle. This is an exciting step because your husband may say, "No, that part doesn't matter to me, it's this that I'm concerned about!" or, "I didn't know that was your reason for doing such and such," etc. That revelation alone is often helpful and leads to better understanding. Having to write down what the problem is forces you to focus on the heart of the matter and clarifies murky verbal communication.

As you show your husband your step 4 solution, ask him if your resolution is acceptable to him. If he doesn't like your solution, brainstorm another one together, or he might have a far better idea. If none of these ideas work, ask him if the two of you could talk further, and if you could pray about it together.

This sort of deep communication is hard work. When tempted to give up, remind yourself that even though the problem isn't a big issue right this minute, it *has* hurt in the past or you wouldn't have been able to write about it. It's worth it to try to iron it out. If there appears to be an impasse at this point, drop it. Go to prayer over it individually. You may think nothing has transpired through this written work, but in the future you may find your spouse more thoughtful or more open in this area—simply because he now is much more aware of how it is impacting you adversely.

6. Be proactive. Don't just internally stew if there is a communication stalemate. <u>Write out a solution for you</u> if your spouse is not going to change on this issue. It must be positive and something you can live with. It must reflect a different way of dealing with the problem than the response you've had in the past. Pray for what this peaceful change in you could be, that will involve adjusting and adapting to the situation as is.

Remember that you may be able to take up this matter again, later, after new evidence presents itself and you've both had more time to pray.

The problem with duking it out verbally over an area of conflict is that in the heat of the moment couples often say things they regret. They escalate. Sadly, this can even begin to feel delicious.

Communication letters without the six steps

Letters to your spouse over conflict areas have many advantages to verbal debates, whether you formally work through all six steps above or just write a letter to communicate. Why are these letters so good?

One: letters are a superb emotion diffuser. They are such a good diffuser that you may find yourself venting all over the paper, only to see how ridiculous the whole thing is and end up tossing the paper into the trash. Think of the wear and tear you just saved your spouse!

Two: letters enable you to accumulate all of your thoughts on a matter without the interruption of dialogue.

Three: writing letters enable you as the wife to sort out and speak from a clear rational head without emotional fog. This in turn lets your man respond to the *issue*, rather than to your emotional packaging.

Four: letter writing eliminates the necessity to battle out an issue as it is happening. You can let it go now because you can write it up later.

Five: writing letters ensures that you won't use downgrading language. Writing allows you to have time to think of encouraging words to include on other matters of your life together.

If, after writing a letter, the issue is not significantly healed, write another and another until you obtain good two-way communication—until your husband is telling you why he is not understanding.

At the end of any letter writing and every tiff, be swift to forgive. Ruth Bell Graham said of marriage, "A happy marriage is the union of two good forgivers." Forgiveness releases objectivity. Perfect the art of forgiveness. Since forgiveness comes more easily where there is greater understanding of the other person's point of view, letters are helpful.

A note: don't save these letters! You're not *documenting* your problems; you're peacefully *identifying* them and working them out.

Write your mate *love* letters, too—at other times—so that every time a white piece of paper comes his way, it is understood that each letter is written only to build up your home—not to tear it down.

A far simpler way to resolve conflict, however, is to wear "rose-colored glasses."

It has been said, "Keep your eyes wide open before marriage, and half shut after!"

Rose-colored glasses are the perfect eyewear for after the "I do." Put them on, and keep them on. The Enemy would have you wear dark sunglasses, shutting out the light of life in marriage by brooding on all of the shadowy parts of your spouse. It is the Enemy's main agenda to get us to dislike each other. The rose-colored glasses defy the dark. They are the perfect tint for a long and happy marriage.

There is enough in every person to make them out to be a demon or a god. It just depends upon which glasses you wear.

12

SECURING YOUR OWN IDENTITY

Identity is tricky in a marriage. You are two, but you are also one. Morally, ethically, and spiritually, you stand alone before God. You will not be judged for your husband's behaviors, nor rewarded for them. You carry your own report card to your Maker. Yet God *makes* the two of you one in other ways in a marriage. You may be one in purpose, one economically, one in joint living conditions and circumstances. And you are certainly one in procreation! To have prenuptial agreements so that you can maintain your own independence is not throwing your weight into the relationship for all of the oneness that God *did* intend. Seeking separateness in finances or not taking his last name is a wrong understanding. Such independence has no place in a lifelong good marriage.

Now let's get a clearer understanding of who holds responsibility for making decisions in a marriage. You, as the wife, are responsible to be absolutely authentic when giving input while you make decisions together. You need to give him your earnest, honest counsel and input, and your exact perceptions. You will not be doing your husband a service to withhold your real counsel from him—no matter how difficult you find it to bring the matter up, initially. You were given to your husband as a helpmeet in *perception*, not just to help with the *practical* work of life. But, as we've said before, after you have offered your input, the husband is responsible before God to make the final decision. If that decision is an unwise one, you will not be held responsible for his defiance against a virtuous path.

Even Pilate's wife said, "Have nothing to do with this Man, I've had hard dreams because of him" (Matthew 27:19). In many cases, a wife can exert a righteous influence over her husband. But in this case, Pilate went right ahead and had a lot to do with this Man. But at the Judgment seat, it's fair to assume she will not be held responsible for those outcomes.

In marriage you are not required to give up your mind/opinions in the name of oneness. You are not required to think your husband's thoughts—under coercion—or to fall under a mental control of an out-of-line, domineering husband. You do not have to accept his negatives about you, or fall under his chronic criticism. You are *free* to get a right view of yourself from a loving God. Your identity is made and upheld by God's love alone. He created you. You are not rubbish. You are valuable beyond all understanding to God.

As God chastens us and grows us, He does it with gentleness and hopefulness, never with a horsewhip or a chronic accusation that never ceases.

Satan is the accuser of the brethren; he is at it day and night. God's refinements don't feel like Satan's. God's sanctifications always have a hidden stair, a way out of temptation, a prodding in right directions, a gentlemanly escort. Learn to discern the difference in your husband's remarks.

Accept God's evaluation of you in prayer. If you are feeling attacked about your identity/value, you have access to God's measurement of you at any moment. Composure about your own worth in God's sight will give you peace amidst conflict. If you are verbally attacked unjustly, you can crawl behind what you know to be true from the Word of God. "Christ died for me. I am His royal child. He loves me unconditionally, forever. He will turn even this painful moment into good for me" (see Romans 8:28).

Learn to entrust your momentary suffering to God. Ruth Graham Bell said, "Beautiful women are made from living with difficult men." Withdraw mentally inside yourself anytime you feel pounded upon by your husband's temporary disgruntlement. Sit in a God-bubble till it passes, but if it remains or seems to be enlarging, confront it before a counselor.

Dealing with temporary harshness or criticalness

Many women have difficulty with critical or harsh husbands, and have a problem knowing how to cope with his recurring negative comments. In some marriages this is a milder dynamic than in others. Many men have some degree of these tendencies. The insightful book, *The Garden of Peace: A Marital Guide for Men Only* by Rabbi Shalom Arush addresses this thoroughly, and will be hugely beneficial for your husband to read in this regard, if this is a problem of his.

Some husbands don't even know they are being harsh, and don't even want to be like that, but find it recurring, even to their own chagrin. Most men have no idea the devastation their wife feels under such comments. The wife *has* to find some way of coping with this to go on thriving as a person. Many women stuff their natural response and then one day yell out, "I want a divorce," and the man is clueless as to why. You must tell him *as you go*. Make him aware of how out of line it is, if this is an increasing dynamic. But not all the time; chalk some of it up to an imperfect human being, and get past it.

If this is your struggle, you will need an emotionally healthy default setting for your own mind. If you are feeling chronically overly criticized by him, remind yourself that you don't have to perform before anybody to be accepted or valued. Joni Erickson Tada certainly can't! She is loved as she is, within marriage. And so are you by God. But once you have established that in your own mind, then go ahead and choose to love your husband ongoingly. Your outside activity and demeanor toward your husband may look exactly the same, but this subtle shift in your thinking will deliver you from the stress caused by another person's untiring perfectionistic agenda for you that, try as you might, you can never measure up to.

If you are trying to earn your husband's love or feel constantly on the performance stage for acceptance from him, this results in a stressful tummy. If you don't change your internal thinking and your own response to these moments, over time your nervous system will burn out. Get the issues clear in your own head and it will free you up immensely— even if your husband does not or cannot change. Empower yourself to choose to love him in spite of his sometimes-thoughtless criticisms. Make it your goal to love unconditionally. *Become* the kind of person to him that you wish your husband were to you.

Because all of us, as wives, are on the road to maturity and have a long way to go, too, if your husband has just criticized you, in a quiet private moment later in prayer, not under duress, ask God if there is truth to the criticism, and ask for His help to overcome it. God will tell you instantly if it stemmed from your husband's own irritability or if this is an area you truly need to work on and to pray through. Examples might be: excessive uncontrolled talking, far too many TV dinners/not supporting your family with very healthy meals, scatteredness, an overloaded schedule, preoccupation with female trivia that will not eternally matter, domineering and drill-sergeant tendencies, your own over the top perfectionisms with your husband and the children, allowing relatives or friends to invade your home and squelch your time with your hubby, etc. We are all in the school of sanctification, and if you can get a little tougher skin you might find that you benefit from your husband's unmeasured responses. Prayer is the great revealer; it is the place of hope, new beginnings, and affirmation. The Devil never gives us such assurances. His style is to hit and run. He accuses us and gives no way out. If you are depressed over these issues, that is not God. Because God's spotlight upon us is filtered by the redemption of the cross, He will benevolently help you to change. Blessed, blessed filter.

Wifely tools to wake up a sluggish hubby

Some husbands are sluggish in their sense of responsibility. Here are four tools a wife can use to help a husband wake up and grow up who had a failure to launch—still absorbed in the adolescent pleasure trap. Some of these husbands are wasting life totally absorbed in video games and/or sports while very real family needs around them are going unmet. Other husbands are trapped in inertia, chronically escaping into the excuse of victimization: "I can't get a job because..." Even if there are no jobs *currently* available, a husband can still work *hard* around your own home as he pursues jobs in *other* cities. In other words, it behooves a husband to be *aggressively* working—either for pay or without pay—and *seeking* pay for his starving family. A feigned helplessness is no answer.

For these cases a wife can use the following tools with her sometimes dysfunctional husband, to eye-opening effect.

1. Place *your* irritation in *his* setting, through word pictures. To help your *rational* husband understand the *emotional* voltage of your issues, reposition the description of them in *his* world, so that it rouses his emotions in his own case enough to match you in yours—i.e., to wake up some empathy. "If your fishin' buddy did that to you over your stuff...Your neighbor undid your discipline with your son...You had an immovable deadline with so and so, and that happened to you...Your boss slighted you just that way," etc.

2. <u>Pit him against himself.</u> Remove yourself from the dilemma entirely. Gently ask him what *he* wants for *his* outcomes in life, even if you didn't exist at all. If he is finding it comfortable to shadow box with you, inferring that you are the source of all of his problems, make him box with himself and his *own* consequences. Where is *he* headed on issue after issue? What sort of outcomes does *he* want to live with the memory of? What sort of relational capital is *he* building for his own old age? What would *he* do with a quadriplegic for a wife, or a mentally retarded child who could give him nothing in return? *Some* men *have* had such needy wives and/or children and been far more content with their lot than perhaps he has with his. Ask him why the difference? Scores of men have dealt better with less favorable circumstances, relatives, finances. Meeting oneself can be eye-opening.

3. <u>Help him identify the escape of victimization in himself.</u> Make sure he has a thorough understanding of the victimization dynamic of using blame as a way of escape from his own self-induced real problems. Entitlement was a disease of the last generation, often resulting in choosing to play over going to work. Our parents and grandparents all *had* to make it financially, no matter what the cost to their brawn and brain, regardless of their starting points.

There is an hour when young adults have to get *past* their past! Blaming their parents, their professors, their lack of money, their lack of opportunity, their birth situation, etc., will not fix their todays. What will their *own* future realities look like, based on their *own current conduct* and decisions? This is called reality therapy. Sigmund Freud *may* find something disastrous in your childhood, but you have a *today* to deal with. Endless diagnosis (lodging blame) is not the issue, decisions and actions from henceforth are. Shifting blame has its waterloo. The cocoon of childhood was never meant to last forever.

4. <u>Boundaries.</u> If your husband is sinfully out of control, you may have to draw some boundaries in your *own* responses. You may have to allow natural consequences to set in. You can tell him at a non-volatile time what *your* boundaries are for when he chooses to do something that is rankly ungodly. For example, if he goes to a bar to get drunk, tell him ahead of time that you will not be available to pick him up at three in the morning. Let him know that he will have to suffer the consequences of his own actions, even if that means he is sent to jail. Let him know that you don't intend to change him, but that you *will* have to set boundaries for *you*—as a consequence of his actions.

Then, when an issue arises, follow through with your previously stated consequences. If you respectfully discussed the inappropriate behavior in the morning and then it erupts at nighttime, say something like, "Remember what we discussed this morning? I can't make you stop yelling at me or foster a desire in you to speak to me nicely. That is your decision, but I will be leaving the room now." "If you want to continue to watch X-rated movies in our home, that is your choice, but the children and I will not be watching them with you. I will be taking them to the other end of the house."

If he is not disciplining the children, you might decide to leave the room for a while and let him see what happens when their behavior goes unchecked. If he is chronically late to appointments, you may have to discuss taking two different cars and using twice the gas. You cannot change him, but you can change your response to him if/when his choices are ungodly or irresponsible.

Marital suffering

Finally, let us look at marital suffering. There are three kinds of suffering that we see in life:

1). Sovereignly allowed suffering (e.g. getting caught in a world war);

2). Suffering caused by our own rashness, deviance, or poor judgment;

3). Suffering resulting from someone else's actions or stumblings.

Much marital suffering falls under this third category. If life were rigged such that people never suffered as a consequence of someone else's choices, then a wife could protest wildly at having to suffer for her husband's chronic or temporary deviant behavior. (Keep in mind that he may be quietly suffering under her behavior, too.) But the cross creates a mild uneasiness in us, that this might not be the case. The prime example of the innocent suffering for the guilty took place on the cross. Our Savior suffered as a consequence of *everyone* else's sin.

In 1 Peter 3 we're told to sit tight in response to suffering as a result of someone else's choices. Suffering is not the end of the line. We may often have to suffer in this life, and this is how we are to cope with it:

"...not returning evil for evil or reviling for reviling, but on the contrary blessing, knowing that you were called to this, that you may inherit a blessing. ... But even if you should suffer for righteousness' sake, you are blessed. 'And do not be afraid of their threats, nor be troubled'" (1 Peter 3:1-2, 9, 14 NKJV).

As we've mentioned, our life may not even be about *us* at some points in the journey. If you find yourself an emotional widow, because of your uncaring husband, turn and get your emotional satisfaction in the LORD. Read Isaiah chapter 54. If your husband is given to moodiness or long bouts of depression, the Lord will be your husband. He will take away the reproach of your widowhood. You can protect and isolate yourself emotionally from your husband's deep valleys, while continuing to love him. Unhook when your husband wants to fight unjustly. A husband can't fight with someone who won't fight back. He may be angry at his job and blame you. But you don't need to meet his need for the adrenaline rush; just walk away. Beware of his button-pushing. Don't take the bait. Play dodgeball. Construct a meaningful inner life based on a rewarding companionship with the LORD. No one can control your thoughts or force you to react in a certain way. Your responses are ultimately a result of your own choices.

This is difficult for a woman, because she is basically a responsive creature. But when you find that your natural response to your husband's sin is destroying you, take mastery over your mind. Prayer will be your lifeline. In torture chambers and concentration camps, victims were ultimately surprised to find that no one could control their mind. (No one can *make* you feel miserable. You allow yourself to feel miserable.) These prisoners were spiritually free, inside themselves, even in chains. If your husband is difficult, it is important—as you find mental survival strategies for yourself, in order to thrive emotionally and spiritually—that you continue to love him as Christ has loved you.

13

KEEP A PRETTY PURSE

Financial stress can wreak havoc in a marriage. Debt is a high marital stressor. Untold numbers of marriages have been shipwrecked solely over this issue. Chronic mismanagement of shared money will come back to sting you.

There is only one true financial formula for success. It has no complicated terms like derivatives, bonds, bankruptcies and rollovers. It is simple and always will be. True fiscal reality, like gravity, will never change. You cannot defy gravity. So here's the timeless winning formula: "Spend less and make more." That's it.

If you are currently in debt, remember the following four principles.

Stop spending. Ben Franklin said a person could become rich by serious adherence to this maxim alone.

Sell off excess. This will be your easiest and fastest money; it will put money in your pocket by nightfall.

Make extra around the edges. Someone or several someones in your family need to start making extra income around the edges. Your family has to start their own *additional* businesses to do in the evenings and weekends while not occupied with wage-earning hours performed for an employer. Hours worked for an employer generally only pay your bills. To get *ahead* you must, for a while, earn extra. The formula has two parts. Frugality is only half of it; entrepreneurialism is the other half.

Carefully manage what you DO make. Save, tithe, and re-invest, ideally in additional ways, for *you* to make more money in your *own* business.

Your single biggest change that can catapult you into greater financial gains is to examine your house payment. No amount of coupon clipping can compare with lowering your mortgage payment or reducing your rent, or getting out of your mortgage altogether. A mortgage is a covenant with death (derived from the Old French words *mort,* "dead," and *gage,* "pledge"). Get out of it if at all possible. There are rapids ahead in the world economy. Head for dry ground now. The more radical you want your future freedoms to be, the more radical must be your decisions today. Living significantly *under* your means is the only way to get ahead. (See our homeschoolhowtos.com website for several financial articles that can give you a big boost in "financial know-how.")

A financially savvy wife is an asset to any man. What goes on in and around her purse and her creative financial ideas can make worlds of difference to the whole family's fortune over the long haul.

WATER

14

POINTS OF CONNECTION

People tend to stay in relationships where they are growing, stimulated, excited, freed up, and nurtured. The opposite dynamic can result in a spouse's exit. If a relationship descends into constantly "being on trial," your mate may contemplate jumping ship. Therefore, you have to major on points of connection to keep your husband chasing you around the house with joy. Plow over the negative and major on the positive if you want to stay in a good marriage. Know for a fact that all office settings, all homes, all public school classrooms, all hospitals, retirement centers, churches, etc., have the potential to be taken over by pirates of negativism. If you don't vault over those dynamics in each of those settings—especially in the context of marriage—you are apt to be thrown overboard and eaten alive, or your spouse may walk the plank himself.

It has been observed that when an elderly spouse dies, the remaining spouse grieves most over those now-missing points of connection. Was it a daily walk together, a favorite dessert, a daily game of chess, prayer times together—what do you do together that will be missed? Are there enough of those points to provide good glue for your marriage?

Connection is all about just being together. Many couples worry that they aren't enough alike. They complain that they have nothing in common, so they begin to think that divorce is inevitable. But historically, widely different personalities have made a tremendous "go" at marriage when they understood this one principle. You don't have to be *anything* alike to have a good marriage. If you are just near one another, in a warm context of some sort sometime during the day, you can remain enormously fulfilled and satisfied. If you, as the wife, are always gone shopping or spending time with girlfriends or away at part-time work or at volunteer civic or church duties, or if your husband is always gone to ball games or hunting, there may not be enough glue in your marriage. You have to be emotionally all there in each other's lives, to provide enough nurture and affirmation to make a marriage work.

Being so different from each other is not the problem, a loss of proximity and emotional bankruptcy is. The husband may go forth to mend fences and the wife go forth to mend socks, but the hugs, gestures of kindness and words of encouragement shared at the intersections of husband and wife during the day are the warm spots that make their jobs worth doing. Increased *caring*, not increased *cloning*, marks the progress of a marriage.

One very busy politician wanted a wife who would just be a soft presence in his life and patter around the house watering the plants in her slippers and brew the coffee. He didn't want a high-octane female version of himself. Conversely, another fellow, who tended to be bored, fell in love with a woman who was "an idea a minute" to give some spunk to his life. Not "likeness" but "presence" is the key. Ponder the example of people who unconsciously grow fond of a lowly cat that they might have despised when it first started begging at their back door. What was the mysterious draw? Familiarity.

Bedding down

Now let's talk about the connecting point of the bed. Bedding down within a marriage is important bonding time. If this is not happening because spouses are sleeping in separate beds or have opposite sleeping times, there may not be enough glue in the marriage. Evening and morning, the bookmarks of the day, have an unconscious intimate dimension to them every day. When we lie down, our bodies switch from alpha waves to theta waves—resulting in more openness with one another. Bed equals bonding. Even tossing and turning together can be bonding. Some couples sleep like spoons together all night, first facing one direction and then the other—turning over in tandem.

So, try to "bed down" together, even if you must separate later in the evening due to hubby's snoring, etc. Begin in bed together and then in the early morning if you happen to be awake, get up and go again to lie with your beloved, so that you rise up together. See to it that you have sufficient horizontal time together. Without the substantial underpinnings that come from laying bricks horizontally to build a good foundation for any building, a building topples.

"Bedding-down-closeness" strengthens your marriage in the same way, and has a language all of its own. This repeated experience is doing both of you far more good than you realize.

This physical tightness is to be found nowhere else in all of life, and it has a subliminal impact on one's total well-being. Little confessions, worries, anxieties, hopes, joys, and reconciliations and touches are expressed in bed in a relaxed way that is a relief to the daily stresses upon personhood. Bedtime is like pulling into port out of the storms of life and laying anchor. It is necessary. It is a daily Sabbath. Things happen while we rest that do not happen in the stream of activity. Going to bed is even a little picture of death and the resurrection. When we go to sleep, we do not even control our own breathing all night long—God does. And while we slumber in each other's arms, the Creator does other things to us over a lifetime, through the marriage bed. If God designed for a pair of animals to lie down in a den together or in a tuft of grass, how much more does he desire it for His people. Adam did not lie down in Paradise while Eve was two hours away in the land of Nod. They were right next to one another, each and every night.

Bed antics

If you are a younger couple and have the energy for it, you can have some outrageously fun athletics in bed, too. Try bicycling backwards with the bottoms of your feet together, in bed. To execute it, you each face opposing walls, back to back, but place the bottoms of your feet together, and then bicycle, moving your legs in a horizontal circle parallel to the bed. Or try bear hugging each other tightly while you roll *together* speedily all the way from one side of the bed to the other. You'll laugh and laugh. In a good marriage, a bed is a safe place to let go. It is only limited by your personalities and what is *mutually* fun and pleasurable.

Conclusion of points of connection

As we've said before, an excellent marriage of two *very* different people who are Believers can always be achieved simply through kindness, alone. Spouses can have nothing in common in their basic personalities, wiring, or even in their hobbies, and still be potentially immensely happy with one another, if kindness rules the day. More points of connection mean more glue. They can be found in: a growing shared spiritual life, children, exercise together, meals together, shared social connections, meaningful domestic projects, shared reading, and classical concerts. Any shared experience is a glue in marriage, despite the distinct and different personalities that the two spouses bring *to* those experiences. It is simply insupportable that we fall out of love because we are too different. We fall out of love because we are too selfish—and have a low reverence/respect tolerance for people who are very different from ourselves.

Our culture has grabbed the Devil's lie that we can't remain together because we have nothing in common. It is the common reason people give for no-fault divorces. But it often is a smoke screen to cover up for the fact that our flesh is adverse to the self-sacrifice needed to make *any* relationship work over the long haul.

The most important glue for marriage is the spiritual. If a couple has the same faith, the same destiny, worships the same God who both made and redeemed them, and reads the same scripture, this is glue indeed. A spiritual life together is the *only* glue actually needed in a marriage. When one originally hunts for a mate, if this glue isn't there, one shouldn't marry. "Do not be unequally yoked together with an unbeliever" (2 Corinthians 6:14). "How can two walk together unless they be agreed?" (Amos 3:3). Such a mismatched couple generally will have a tougher time of making the relationship last. The low-grade pain will begin the morning after the honeymoon. "The couple that prays together stays together." However, if this division happens *after* marriage, there are all kinds of sovereign graces available to the one who became a Believer, to make it work.

And, of course the very opposite of connectedness is adultery. Here is how to guard against it for both hubby and wife.

How to reduce your husband's risk of temptation to be unfaithful

Be his cheerleader, his best fan, and his "main squeeze." Meet his physical needs. The Scriptures say, "Do not deny one another, except for a season of prayer" (1 Corinthians 7:5). And feed the guy. Lots!

How to reduce your risk of temptation to be unfaithful as a wife.

First, recognize that there are two dogs in all of us: the one who likes to walk the straight and narrow, and the other who likes to prance the boardwalk.

Which dog do you feed? Romance novels and soap operas feed the wrong dog. They will flood your mind with comparisons, and will produce death in your marriage.

The real daily life walked with God, believe it or not, has a better glory to it than any earthly substitutes. God's plan for you and your marriage is far more exciting than what is packed between two paper covers gotten at a convenience store or between the hours of one and two in the afternoon off a TV screen. "Eye has not seen, nor ear heard, neither has it entered into the heart of man what God has prepared for those who love Him" (1 Corinthians 2:9). Romance novels and soap operas are mere tinsel in comparison.

Secondly, conversation, not sex, leads to adultery. That is why adultery happens so often between bosses and secretaries. The daily casual talks and checking in with one another opens the door for trouble. If there is some man in your life who you find very easy to talk with, cut it off. Needing to talk things over with him continuously is cause for alarms and bells and whistles. It is continuous conversation that leads the way to adultery. It might be a neighbor, a doctor, a pastor, a grocery store clerk, a mentor, a teacher. Go out of your way to choose another way home. Move. Change seats. Change churches. Who knows which conversation could crack your family tree? Future generations will call you blessed.

Here's another practical suggestion. If you are tempted with an adulterous thought, just draw near to your own husband. Look toward him and do something extra loving for him, right at the moment. If you do, you'll find that moment of temptation will scurry away, embarrassed that it couldn't find a place to roost in your heart.

15

ROMANCE YOUR MAN

A cheerful countenance says it all. Go ahead. Snarl up. Get a good head of steam on an angry countenance. Stop in the middle of an argument sometime. Freeze the look on your face, hurry and go look at the mirror. Isn't it ghastly! Then let it slowly and gently dawn upon you how many times your husband has seen you look like that. Ouch! Is that the last image you want your husband to have as he goes off on an errand?

How many women do you know who consistently have a cheerful countenance imprinting on their hubby's memory? We could probably count them on one hand. Remember, your husband doesn't *have* to love you. He *could* just endure you. We need to see to it that we are so pleasant to live with that they would feel bereft without us.

Here's a revealing exercise. Ask yourself, "Would I want to be married to *me*? If I were a man, what would I want in a wife?" Go ahead. Make a list. I bet a home-cooked dinner every night would be on there. A cheerful countenance. A calm and

gentle spirit. Whew! Are you any of those things?
A cheerful countenance is a choice. If you make
yourself do it for 30 days, you'll be well on your way
to the habit.

Choose to cultivate a grateful heart and smile
more. When you do, watch the reaction of your
mate. You can quell nearly any raging tide by cheerfulness; change the whole course of the day, for that
matter!

Good grooming matters, too. Pick the right
colors to wear, no matter how inexpensive or casual
the outfit. A color that matches your coloring will
make you look fresh and young; the wrong color will
make you look cross, whether you are or not! Try
not to wear dowdy clothes. Your family is stuck
with you all day. Why not look as pleasant as possible? It's a gift to them. This does not mean acquiring expensive clothes—just wearing the right colors
is all it takes. If a color makes you look worn-out,
throw it out. Wear clothing that is feminine, but
modest. Some husbands like the feel of certain fab-
rics, too. Bottom line: if you look like a lady, your
husband will find himself treating you like a lady.
Just watch!

Create an uplifting semantic atmosphere. Catch
your husband up in it. Great exploits are started by
the power of words. Defeats are overcome, tempta-
tions dashed, endurance won, and people made—all
by words. A liberal use of positive words weaves a
special power for good upon your man.

Be contented with your circumstances, and speak
that contentment to your husband while in each situation. If you live in difficult circumstances, create a
life "within" those circumstances that makes him

want to rush home to you. Chronic complaining will wear a man's spirit down and make him turn from you inwardly.

If at all possible, try to avoid taking a job outside of the home. All too often a woman's boss becomes her new husband, psychologically. She winds up showing him more respect than she does her husband. And when these women find themselves juggling balls, the *home* ball will always be the one to drop—never the job.

Cultivate a gentle and quiet spirit. It's supernatural, of course. Beg God for it. The Bible says in 1 Peter 3:4 that it is of great worth in God's sight. God probably picked Mary to be the Messiah's mother partially because of it. Ponder it.

Be playfully romantic at dull times. Find something funny to squeeze from the situation. Plan some happy event for someone else in need—together. Use humor to dispel a quarrel. Use a loving tone of voice; be gentle in demeanor. Constantly work at lowering the timbre of the sound of your voice. High-pitched voices wear a husband out. Shakespeare pointed it out when he wrote, "Her voice was ever soft and low—an excellent thing in a woman" (*King Lear*). Say only positive things about him in front of others, and downright *brag* on him in front of his parents and siblings.

"Loving *touch*" is to a man what "loving *words*" are to a woman. When you're prone to be indifferent in the bedroom, remind yourself that woman was created *for* man, not the other way around (Genesis 1:22). This is a vital part of what you were created for. You nourish the man in some profound, unseen way by your loving response in this area.

It has been said that a woman's largest sex organ is her mind (actually, the same is true for the man). So, focus; be attentive; be there. Don't just show up; throw your heart into it, and he'll not be tempted to look elsewhere! Sadly, someone once told us of a relative who left his wife after 47 years of marriage because of continuous sorrow in this area. As someone said, "The Devil works so hard to get us to have sex wrongfully before marriage and then works overtime to keep us apart, or indifferent after marriage."

When you're not quite "up-to-it" you may want to re-negotiate a better time for both of you, a time he can count on—and make sure you follow through. Remember that a woman is capable of great self-sacrifice for her children; her devotion should be no less for her husband.

Because eating is so important to your man, plan and prepare. Even if it is very simple, try to know what you are having for dinner before breakfast is done. A weekly plan will keep you on track. If you'll make dinner first thing in the morning you'll feel like a free woman the rest of the day. Something as simple as a man's repeatedly dashed expectations over dinner can sabotage a marriage.

To help you get serious about feeding him, make it one of your highest priorities rather than your last priority. Set aside your own projects to first serve him. Remember that steady persevering work at the daily round of duty is blessed in the kingdom of God. The only way to endure the daily round is to elevate it! Do the menial task with excellence and uncommon beauty. Run out to meet *it*, before it buries *you*! Stay ahead of the necessary routines of the home to reduce panic and domestic guilt. Do it all with your eye upon the Master and he'll give you the necessary energy time and again. We are most like Him when we serve.

HARVEST

16

CONCLUSION

To have a successful marriage, in summary, never lose sight of the fact that you are imperfect and your spouse is imperfect, and that marriages never arrive, they just grow. Remember that, try as you might, you'll never understand it all. There is much about marriage that remains a mystery.

Even though it takes energy, try to communicate steadily and ongoingly. Don't trust mental telepathy. Help your husband understand you, and seek to understand him.

Major on points of connection and good will. Keep your marriage dominated by the positives, instead of the conflicts, even if you have to pull way back on communicating authentically. Don't upset that positive side of the equation. Let it remain the stronger side for the great majority of the time that you dwell together.

Grow in demonstrating caring ways and manners in your private life with your husband, regardless of whether it is returned or not. Do it for your own dignity as a human being. Grow better and better at expressing this sort of love via 1,000 quiet self-denials.

Cherish an emerging soul. Thank God for your ringside seat of viewing the sacred progress of another person over a lifetime. These close-up observations give you insights about your own humanity. Seek to provide a kind environment—a harbor within your own person for the safe growth of another. Strive to be a lover for all seasons to one man. It is an occupation and a vocation with no regrets.

TODD ELLISON'S LETTERS TO HUSBANDS

How to dwell with your wife according to knowledge

Dear Men,

I know from experience that at times your wife can seem confusing to you, especially when contrary messages and emotions seem to be coming out of her. She can seem like a puzzle.

One of the most significant core issues for a husband is that he needs to learn to validate his wife's feelings. This seems like a waste of time to most of us who want to get on with the issue at hand and not bother with her fluctuating, often erratic, and seemingly unreasonable emotions. But what men find is that if they don't take the time to do a good job with handling their wife's fragile and real emotions, it can take up inordinate amounts of *more* time after letting it fester. Since we, as men, are goal-oriented, understand it this way: you *will* spend time with your wife's emotions; the *amount* of time you will spend on it depends upon how you value her at the moment, in the fray. It is expedient for us to deal with her gently at the time; it is in our own *self-interest*—to say nothing of how it shows how much we value her.

You will find that she is often quite adaptable and cooperative after she has been validated in her feelings. A woman's feelings are not trifling matters. Because she is a responsive creature (even in her anatomy) she can't help her feelings; they are part of her God-given wiring. A man may choose to ignore her feelings, check out while she is expressing them, roll his eyeballs, discount them, or criticize her, but if he does, he will grow a ticking time bomb.

The Scriptures say that a husband is to dwell with his wife "according to knowledge" (1 Peter 3:7). Since every woman is different, this means he has to *study* his particular wife and apply himself to learning all he can about how his own wife ticks. What stresses her? What causes her small anxieties? What is she genuinely thrilled with at her core—not just pretending to like or adapt to? Knowing her well helps you hit the bull's-eye of having a happy responsive wife. You'll miss the mark if you don't study your wife. Stereotypes and cultural norms and Valentine's Day trinkets can't help you. You have to learn to read your wife.

Hit the mark with your wife in as many details as you are able. Don't give her flowers and poems if she'd far prefer that the kitchen faucet drip be fixed. Stay away from giving the daring negligee or jewelry if she'd rather have had a thoughtfully selected book. Don't take her to a lecture on agriculture when she'd rather be listening to one on history. Finding out what lights your wife's fire or what throws cold water on it is far more important than you realize.

This old song sums up our challenge as husbands:

> *If I loved ya like the way I want to love ya,*
> *I fear it would be just what I'd like for **me**.*
> *But somethin' tells me I'd be lovin' you poorly.*
> *What means the most to **you**, I long to be.*

If she is a gourmet cook and you only let her buy rice, she gets locked up inside. Find another area to be frugal in, but let her out of *your* box in *her* areas. If she is anxious about social impressions, time pressures, discipline with the children, etc., take note, overly compensate, and diffuse the levels of anxiety connected with her stresses in every area where you observe it. Shoulder the stress.

Do frequent check-ups to make sure you've not put her into a pressure cooker (that you may be oblivious to). Listen to her feelings and *validate* them. She does not want answers or solutions. She wants to be counted in the marriage. If you shut down while she is exposing her thought life to you, it will cost *you* later, when her feelings surface in further problems.

Because women *do* have expectations, one way for you to keep your marriage loving and healthy is by frequently asking (or reminding yourself of) these two questions: "Is there any job I've left undone? Anything to be fixed?" and "Have I hurt you in any way?"

Your wife needs communication like you need sex. Furthermore, communication is more than talking—just as sex is more than a man shooting his wad. If you don't allow for daily communication, it will take far more time to sort out your wife's stock-piled feelings later. You can't take shortcuts in this area without paying for them.

At first you'll feel clumsy at all this, but over time you'll become more accurate, eyeing a speck of dust in the works, before it clogs the gears.

Your reward for quietly observing her stresses, anxieties, real likes and dislikes? She will become your own personal fan club. If you will take your wife's personhood seriously, she will feel safe with you. She will grow to genuinely prefer you over all other people on the globe. If you study the God-given gem that she is, she will become lovingly responsive to you, and your experience of studying her will grow in you a maturity toward all people. You'll have become Christ-like and you won't even know when it happened.

Sincerely,
Todd

P.S. Here are six phrases men can use to achieve a fabulous marriage. Sent to me by a brother who has a great marriage and a good sense of humor:

I love you.	*You look great!*
Can I help?	*It's my fault.*
Let's eat out tonight!	*Tell me about it.*

A responsive woman vs. a recovering woman:
. A hidden key to your wife!

Dear Men,

Here is a surprising idea for a man about sex. Whether a man is having sex with a prostitute or his wife, most men are having sex with a *recovering* woman, not a *responsive* woman. Many men have no idea of the depth of what they are missing with their wives by not having a firm grasp of this point. Men often think that what they are experiencing in the sexual area with their wives is all there is. But they are kept out of a deeper experience in the same way that their car can't go through a concrete wall. They are kept out by a lack of a simple yet profound understanding. There *is* good ground on the other side—the man just can't get to it. Here is why.

A man is built by God—both in his physical prowess and in his psyche—to be an *initiator*. Conversely, a woman is built—both in her physical prowess and *especially* in her psyche—to be a *responder*. As a result, a man's every little action and word matters. According to Ken Nair (marriage counselor and well-known author of *Discovering the Mind of a Woman*), a woman is a hopeless responder! She can *determine* to have a better response, *resolve* to have a better response, *reason* to have a better response, *plan* a better response to her husband's next critical word (even if it is said only seconds after her lofty internal pep talk), but as soon as he makes the remark, her resolute "house of cards of resolve" collapses. Why? Because she is a responder. She can't help it. When a man understands this fact about a woman it can alter the destiny of his sexual experience, to say nothing of his fuller all-day life with his wife, dramatically.

A woman opens up in her body in direct proportion to the degree that she opens up in her heart. The key to a woman's body is her *heart!* A woman responds primarily to one key thing in a man. It is not good looks, intelligence, hard work, chore-sharing, strength, or popularity, as likeable as these qualities are. Any man can win his woman's heart through the use of *one* thing that will absolutely slam-dunk the deal and get the couple past any obstacle: kindness.

Solomon said there were four things he couldn't understand. One of them was "the way of a man with a maid" (Proverbs 30:19 NASB). A husband can masterfully woo his wife to the state where he totally short-circuits her mind. She is out there in the stratosphere and her body then *follows*, letting loose in response to his physical touch.

However, what happens is that at any time during the day that a man has used a curt word with his wife, or purposefully ignored her, or slighted her or criticized her, no matter how small the remark, she *retreats*, *retracts*, and *recoils* at deep levels to *protect* herself. And if this is a chronically recurring dynamic, she never totally lets down that guard. Enter the sexual experience. The man is having sex with a recovering woman, a "for now" boarded-up woman. She is a *fenced-off* woman, at *some* level. She is *still* in protection mode. It takes her hours and sometimes *days* to let that guard down, after each episode. As a woman, she *has* to do this, to survive—just like the way a morning glory blossom closes up against the night. Try as you might, you can't get that thing open unless you destroy the petals in the attempt—in which case the flower won't open up the next day either. Both the morning glory and the woman are "respond-a-thons" to the cold—made that way in their very essence, by God. They don't have physical strength, so they come to rely on their psychological strength just to breathe free under duress.

The case is the same with a prostitute. She knows that she was used by a man before, so there is no way that the next man gets a full experience. He gets *something*, but it isn't *unity*. She is a *recovering* woman, not a *responsive* one. It is what made Amnon hate Tamar afterwards (2 Samuel 13). He knew that her heart wasn't in it. A warm, fully responsive woman (and only a loved wife can achieve this state) is won by continued kindness. A consistently kind husband is then rewarded by a lasting confidence of oneness and sexual happiness at his core.

Kindness opens up a wife. It is the only path to get her fully open. If the kindness is intermittent—wonderfully expressed today but irritated tomorrow—she withdraws. She comes "out" to the direct degree that her sureness grows that he will have a steady, dependable, caring way with her. The key is simple. But it will require a man to exercise self-denial and grow in a seasoned and ever-deepening maturity. If you think the case if overstated, just ask your wife.

Sincerely,
Todd

A Story: Adam's Barter with God (author unknown)

Did you hear how it went in the garden between Adam and God? Adam was out walking in the cool of the day when he realized that he was lonely. He said, "LORD, please make a helpmeet for me."

The Creator answered back, "Adam I've been aware that you are lonely for some time and I've got something in mind. I will make you a helpmeet who will fulfill your wildest fantasies before you ever even dream them up. She'll be a ravishing beauty; she'll never sag after childbirth. She'll wash your feet every evening; she'll never have PMS. She'll speak sweetly at all times—never question your judgment or utter a cross word. She'll wipe the sweat from your brow and shower you with encouragement. She'll be ready with a well-cooked meal each evening and have the children scrubbed and obedient ready to honor you when you walk through the door."

And Adam said, "Wow, LORD, that sounds swell, but how much would something like that cost me? It sounds too good to be true." And God answered back "Well, Adam, the way I figure it, that'll cost you an arm and a leg."

Adam thought it over and then said in a bit of a sweat, "LORD, I fear that's too steep for me," then brightened up with another thought and said, "How much could I get for a rib?!"

RECOMMENDED READING

For men: *The Garden of Peace: A Marital Guide for Men Only*, by Rabbi Arush

For women: *Women: A Stumbling Identity*, by Renée Ellison (at www.homeschoolhowtos.com)

For over 100 more works and scores of insightful blogs by Renée Ellison, visit

http://homeschoolhowtos.com/